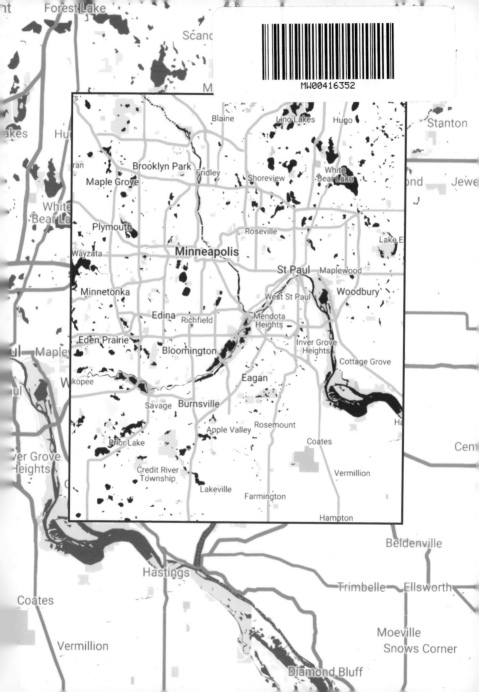

TWIN CITIES
COCKTAILS

AN ELEGANT COLLECTION OF OVER 100 RECIPES INSPIRED BY MINNEAPOLIS & ST. PAUL

PETER SIEVE, MOLLY EACH, MECCA BOS

CIDER MILL
PRESS

BOOK
PUBLISHERS

TWIN CITIES COCKTAILS

ISBN-13: 978-1-64643-417-6
ISBN-10: 1-64643-417-X

This book may be ordered by mail from the publisher. Please include $5.99 for postage and handling. Please support your local bookseller first!

Books published by Cider Mill Press Book Publishers are available at special discounts for bulk purchases in the United States by corporations, institutions, and other organizations. For more information, please contact the publisher.

Cider Mill Press Book Publishers
"Where good books are ready for press"
501 Nelson Place
Nashville, Tennessee 37214
cidermillpress.com

Typography: Rumble Brave, Avenir, Copperplate, Sackers, Warnock

Photography credits on page 359

Printed in India

24 25 26 27 28 REP 5 4 3 2 1

First Edition

CONTENTS

Introduction · 4

An Abridged History of Modern Craft
Cocktails in the Twin Cities · 14

Anatomy of a Cocktail: An in-depth look
into the evolution of a drink,
and the philosophy behind it · 20

Stocking Your
Minnesota Bar · 30

Minneapolis · 34

St. Paul · 170

The Suburbs · 202

Distilleries · 228

The Innovators: a look at the people
who have pushed the Twin Cities
cocktail scene to the next level—and
continue to move it forward · 282

Iconic Destinations and Legendary
Dive Bars · 338

The Local Favorites: Waxing
Poetic About the Twin Cities'
Essential Cocktails · 348

About the Authors · 356

Acknowledgments · 357

Measurement Conversions · 358

Index · 360

INTRODUCTION

The Back Bar at Young Joni (see page 160)

'm a bar person. Always have been. And if you're cracking open this book, I'm guessing you are, too. I'll eschew a table any day, in any place that has the option, for a bar or counter spot. I want to be in the mix, overhearing back-of-house banter, catching the knowing looks between bartenders and waitstaff, watching the craft happen in real time—so much of it casually but expertly performed, in the quietly poetic way muscle memory works. The bar is where the action is.

This book is ostensibly about craft cocktails, in the same way that *Meal Magazine*—the print magazine that my co-authors Mecca Bos and Molly Each and I occasionally publish here in the Twin Cities—is ostensibly about food. The stories we tend to find interesting almost always end up having less to do with the food on the plate or the drink in the glass, and much more to do with the people behind it—the endlessly fascinating dance between those who consume and those who produce the stuff we eat and drink.

Like any creation, a cocktail can be elegiac or prosaic; poetry or piss; a complex story unfolding in a coupe, or a simple, blunt-force tool to get a job done. Cocktail culture in the Twin Cities is a messy and delightful Venn diagram of draft Old Style in a dimly lit dive, liquid sculptures adorned with feathers and poured in million-dollar rooms, patio Bloodies on a blistering summer Sunday brunch (or spiked hot bevvies around a fire in the dark depths of winter), and

Riva Terrace at Four Seasons Hotel Minneapolis (see page 140)

concoctions designed by forager-lab-rat eccentrics doing some of the most innovative things in the nation.

But in the end, a drink isn't much on its own. It's nothing without a hand to hold it, some kind words exchanged across it, and a mouth to sip it. Something about trees falling in forests, hearing them or not . . . that old chestnut.

That's why we, the editors of *Meal Magazine*, naturally gravitated to the stories of the bartenders and artists behind the drinks and why they make them, who in turn often told us the tales of the people behind them who produce the things the bartenders use, and on and on this wonderful dance goes.

Let's dive in with a truth that often goes unsaid when we rhapsodize about cocktails and bar culture, just so we're all on the same page here: ethanol is really fucking bad for us. We know this, and we rarely speak of it. That is a long and fascinating enough conversation on its own, but the growing awareness of this simple fact is having a major

impact on how we're even defining cocktails here in the Twin Cities—
historically an epicenter of the recovery community. Plenty of the
most considered and delicious cocktails, beers, wines, and other beverages are beginning to contain no alcohol at all. These innovators
aren't just creating N/A drinks: they're normalizing the culture to include those who don't imbibe, allowing them to take part in every
aspect of human social life that is soaked in booze—without having to
resort to a club soda or bottle of O'Doul's.

Take Marigold, the city's first N/A bottle shop. Honeycomb Salon
owner Erin Flavin opened it after she became sober during the pandemic. She began stocking all of the locally-produced N/A beverages
she could find right next to the styling creams, shampoos, and condi-
tioners. Now, Marigold is its own bright, airy, dedicated space, with
shelves filled with mocktails, nonalcoholic wines, and other high-qual-
ity N/A products.

"I need it, and other people need it," says Flavin. "The open arms
that this city has brought to us, god, it's so awesome to see. I love
being able to give people things that make them feel better . . . and it's
so fun to see how much this touched the community as a whole."

This inclusivity aperture has been expanding in other meaningful
ways, too—especially since the twin traumas of the pandemic and the
sickening murder of a man named George Floyd on the streets of
Minneapolis by our very own police force. Both events created pro-
found ripple effects across the world, and the aftermath of Floyd's killing had our local institutions—including bars and restaurants—spinning,
forcing us to take a hard look at what we're doing, how we're doing it,
and why. How can we all show up better for each other?

It became glaringly apparent that we all needed to elevate voices
who have been historically written into the margins of this industry, if
not off the page entirely; namely women, Black and Indigenous folks,
and other people of color. Today, these voices are louder than ever in

the drinking and dining scene, to everyone's benefit. In our most highly visible example, owners Sean Sherman and Dana Thompson won Best New Restaurant at the 2022 James Beard Awards for their landmark Indigenous restaurant Owamni—and their bar program serves wine, beer, and spirits made exclusively by BIPOC producers.

"Alcohol has a very colonial, capitalistic history," says Sherman. "It's super evident how little diversity there is, because alcohol production is all about land access."

The history of Black hospitality spaces—in particular the amazing story of Minnesota's first Black bar owner, A.B. Cassius, included in this book—reveals what many of us have swept under the cultural rug but knew to be true: despite our reputation for "Minnesota Nice," the upper Midwest has had its own ways of marginalizing people of color that have been just as destructive as the old Jim Crow laws of the South. That's changing due to the hard work of many, and with advocacy from strong voices and business owners like Minneapolis distiller Chris Montana of Du Nord Social Spirits (the first Black-owned distillery in Minnesota). "We've always been focused on craft spirits and quality in the bottle, but we've never been about just making money," says Montana. "We want to show up in ways that matter for other people."

Today in the Twin Cities, the hospitality scene has changed dramatically, and cocktails and bars along with it. We lost some dedicated cocktail rooms like Marvel Bar during the pandemic. New ventures have cropped up, many with a smaller, more neighborhood-scaled focus. Drinks are still made with serious drive and focus, but increasingly, the pretention balloon has all but popped, and we're emphasizing people over products. Hospitality, always a strong suit, is even more of a priority, and bartenders, chefs, owners, and others are questioning the old ways of working to come up with more sustainable ways to not just survive, but thrive.

Collaboration, mutual support, and knowledge-sharing is the norm, and a heavy turn toward Minnesota terroir has jumped from dining to drinks. Bartenders are working hand in hand with chefs, farmers, foragers, academics, and others to identify how we can best express our region in a glass, and how to simultaneously move away from importing most of our flavor building blocks. What happens when our expectations for what has to be in a Negroni get challenged, and our palates expanded, by what we start discovering and embracing in our own backyard to express similar—better?—experiences, not only agriculturally, but culturally?

"I have this theory of what I call cultural gravity," says Pip Hanson, who opened Marvel Bar in 2011 and now heads up the bar program at O'Shaughnessy Distilling Co. "It's basically the idea that when a metro area gets a certain amount of mass as represented by population, it stops losing and starts attracting—like a planet. Everyone has that moment in Minneapolis here and there where we're like, man, I wish

Sidebar at Surdyk's (see page 146)

this city was twice as large! I wish we could just get some late-night dumplings somewhere! But you can see what's happening anywhere in the culinary world from your phone. Suddenly you're running out of reasons to start sharpening your elbows in, say, San Francisco," he says. "Suddenly it makes a lot more sense: we've got farmland here where we can grow all the raw materials we need.

"And now that a guy like Brian Nation [master distiller at O'Shaughnessy Distilling in Minneapolis, formerly of Jameson] is here, or Sean Sherman, or our Hmong scene, our Somali scene—we've got some cultural Venn diagrams that overlap. I think it means we have some interesting ideas that will come out of here that are not just Francophile. It doesn't have to be the huge buzzy, expensive, hyped restaurants. I think we're refocusing what our definition of 'premium' is."

What's happening now in the Twin Cities cocktail scene is thrilling. The collective energy and invention is leading to exciting and unpredictable things, and opening doors that were previously shut. The future is impossible to hold in our hands, but in the present, we can

cradle a glass of something that was crafted thoughtfully in the recent past, and enjoy it right now. It might be a complex cocktail made of Minnesota-grown and distilled spirits and botanicals, a bottle of celebratory zero-proof wine, a draft beer and a bump at the neighborhood dive, or whatever creative concoction someone right here, right now, in this creative, supportive cocktail culture, is coming up with next.

But in the end, the drink itself is the least important thing. It's a reason to gather, build relationships, strengthen community, and develop the bonds we have with each other, our land, and the way we work and play together. The drink is fleeting, suspended for mere moments in reformed silica before disappearing down our gullet. It's a labor of love, something for us to do as the real work of living life happens daily: spending time with people we care about, celebrating the present moment as it arrives, and savoring this complicated and sometimes beautiful existence.

Our modest editorial team here at *Meal Magazine* has done our level best to gather some of the most consequential voices in this little volume to give you just a glimpse of what's happening in this vibrant scene. Please read on, and dive deeper into the valuable perspectives and recipes from some of the best in the world, right here in the Twin Cities.

—Peter Sieve

AN ABRIDGED HISTORY OF MODERN CRAFT COCKTAILS IN THE TWIN CITIES
by Joy Summers

It's been interesting to watch cocktail culture swing from pour-and-serve basics to the modern era of obscure or small-batch spirits in the Twin Cities. In the early aughts, Chino Latino—a trendy Asian-fusion restaurant in Uptown Minneapolis—started putting dry ice, dendrobium orchids, and tiny plastic monkeys in a glass that debuted when the national Cosmo craze was happening thanks to *Sex and the City*.

Somewhere around that time, in 2006, restaurateur Tim Niver handed Nick Kosevich an ice cream blender inside the newly-opened Town Talk Diner. In the Twin Cities, there was pre- and post-Town Talk, which only lasted for a few years. That was a catalyst moment when being a bartender went from something you did for tips to a respected career path. People started passing around cocktail books, and really studying the early drinks. Soon the Dale DeGroff Daiquiri started popping up on menus.

Dan Oskey emerged at the Strip Club [a cheekily-named St. Paul steak house], not coincidentally another Tim Niver-helmed restaurant. Oskey was the first person I met who was making his own homemade tonic. He could nerd out for hours about the chemistry happening in the glass, but was also one of the most skilled bartenders in reading a room and meeting a customer where they were. It was so fun to drink there.

The Lexington (see page 190)

Meanwhile, across town, Johnny Michaels was giving cocktails rockstar poet names and training an entire generation of cocktail makers at La Belle Vie. He even wrote a book about it, called *North Star Cocktails: Johnny Michaels and the North Star Bartenders' Guild*, which really broke the cocktail world here wide open. Everyone had that book, and it was a source of pride for everyone who had a recipe printed inside it.

There were hotbeds of talent like Bradstreet Crafthouse that were doing those huge spheres of clear ice before that became normal. Saffron [the downtown Palestinian fine dining spot by chef Sameh Wadi] wasn't where you'd expect to find huge bar talent—the bar was so small—but they were there. That was also an early place to find the same care put into spiked drinks as well as N/A drinks. Cafe Maude was a quiet neighborhood place that also turned out a ton of talent. Trish Gavin was having a lot of fun making appealing bitter drinks at Heidi's.

Then there was Pip Hanson, coming in with this incredible depth of knowledge and an entirely different approach after apprenticing in Japan in 2011. His work at Marvel Bar was another seismic shift. Now, bartenders weren't just rakes determined to keep the party moving— they were taste aficionados who might know as much about single-origin coffee and Nietzsche as what was being poured in the glass. For a while, that was the most bookish, intensely curious bar staff in the city.

Eat Street Social was the first place I know of where the bartenders constructed the actual bar, using sushi coolers to keep garnishes fresh. That was where I first met Marco Zappia, lighting things on fire and generally being the curious kid in the room reading all the things and tinkering with really basic concepts to come up with revolutionary answers.

And then Jesse Held opened Parlour, where a lot of what had been bubbling up around town converged in one solid drink spot that almost acted as a proving ground for a new generation of bar talent.

The current era has been fascinating, because we went from all this growth and study and knowledge to master and reinvent the Prohibition-era classic cocktails, and now there's an uncertainty as to what comes next. Some bars are really digging into zero waste—cutting out citrus, for example, and replacing it with magnesium citrate. Others are trying to modernize some of those old 1980s cocktails, and the jury's still out on whether or not that's going to work. N/A cocktails are truly growing up and exploding in all kinds of ways. THC is dropping into the party. It's wild.

Can Can Wonderland (see page 181)

ANATOMY OF A COCKTAIL:

by Marco Zappia

AN IN-DEPTH LOOK INTO THE EVOLUTION OF A
DRINK, AND THE PHILOSOPHY BEHIND IT

MARCO ZAPPIA OF 3LECHE, IN HIS OWN WORDS

I fell in love with a girl when I first came back to Minnesota. She was a dancer and worked part time as a host at a little restaurant in Northeast Minneapolis. I decided the way to win her heart was to apply and work near her. I started out in dish/busboy, worked my way up the ranks, and when the owners decided to open another location called Eat Street Social with a full liquor license, I jumped at the chance to learn how to bartend. That's where I met my first bar mentors and got hooked on tending stick.

When I first met the girl, she was dating a bartender at a now-closed Minneapolis spot that had a drink on the menu called the Naked Ballerina. They eventually broke up, she and I started dating, and we fell in love. Being a 19-year-old little shit, I decided to work on a cocktail called Naked Ballerina #2. It was my first cocktail to make it onto a menu—there's no way to describe how good that moment feels.

Here's my original recipe.

EAT STREET SOCIAL NAKED BALLERINA #2

RINSE: Absinthe
GLASSWARE: Martini glass
GARNISH: Marigold or peacock feather

- Fat ¾ oz. Cazadores Reposado Tequila
- ¾ oz. Cocchi Americano Rosa
- Skinny ¾ oz. orange liqueur
- ¾ oz. lemon
- ¼ oz. simple syrup (1:1)
- Dash Bittercube Jamaican #1 Bitters

Shake, strain.

Looking at it closely, it's quite representative of modern bartending. The philosophy developed by Sasha Petraske (of Milk & Honey fame) gave bartenders creative license to take classic cocktails and play "Mr. Potato Head" with the ingredients; ratios over recipes, nothing is sacred. *The Cocktail Codex* by Alex Day, Nick Fauchald, and David Kaplan is the best book to explain the modern ideology—I won't go into it in too much detail, but the Naked Ballerina is simply a riff on the Corpse Reviver #2. It's tasty.

MARTINA NAKED BALLERINA #2

After my stint at Eat Street Social, I worked as a partner in a bitters company, consulting on a masochistic number of bar openings. Fast-forward a few. I came back to Minnesota for the second time and teamed up with chef Daniel del Prado to open Martina. This would be the first time releasing a program that was all mine, with nothing to hide behind. It was extremely nerve-wracking and exciting. Who was I, and what did I want to say? I updated the Naked Ballerina #2 and brought it back for the opening menu, like this:

GLASSWARE: Coupe, sidecar
SPRITZ: Calamansi, absinthe
GARNISH: Peacock feather

- ◆ 20 ml lemon
- ◆ 15 ml passion fruit/vanilla syrup
- ◆ 45 ml blanco tequila blend
- ◆ 15 ml rosa vermouth
- ◆ 10 ml orange liqueur
- ◆ 2 dashes Peychaud's bitters

20 ml lemon, 75 ml pre-batch, shake, strain, garnish.

So what changed this time? Instead of listing the brands of liquor, we decided to blend all of our spirits. This accomplished two things: we dropped our cost of goods by purchasing cases of 1750 ml bottles from the larger houses, allowing us to sneak in higher-priced local spirits that would normally be too expensive. This practice also kept us out of the "pay-to-play" shenanigans I had been privy to during my earlier years, keeping cocktails pure by removing any possibility for menu placement. We made all of our own liqueurs, vermouths, and bitters in house; the more autonomous of a program we could be, the better.

You'll also notice milliliter measurements instead of ounces, as God intended. Ingredients are listed cheapest to most expensive for specs, getting smarter on financials. The instruction evolution is cool to check out, too: when opening Martina, we took over an existing restaurant with a bar that only had two wells. It was very much lacking in space, considering the volume we were pushing out. Thus, the full-on *à la minute* jiggering we did at Eat Street Social turned into cheater bottles at Martina, blending shelf-stable ingredients into one bottle which streamlined the pickup to a two-step build (batch plus citrus juice). This practice is now nearly universal in Minneapolis restaurant bars, and a lot of programs take it a step further by batching the citrus component as well. It's not necessarily a bad thing—our Twin Cities restaurant bars are amazing and doing some of the coolest programs in the country. Batching in totality allows the director to increase the artistic and creative components, the team can direct more bandwidth to hospitality, and overall deliver the wow factor in volume. The one hang-up is that there's no opportunity to really make mistakes with batched cocktails, which is such an important part of a round education: messing up and learning from it. The best way to learn the craft component of bartending is building *à la minute*—technician first, artist second.

I don't remember why I added passion fruit to Martina's recipe. Thirst trap?

Fast-forward to COVID-19 popping off in 2020, and we started a new business! I had always wanted to become a producer in the three-tier system, romantically dreaming of being able to touch every single point of the journey from raw materials, ferment, spirit, and finally the crescendo of the cocktail. Our incubator, which we call 3LECHE, would be the vehicle to birth bar commissary, pantry/larder, and other eclectic exploratory brands. We'd create paint and brushes for the bartenders, chefs, and hospitality professionals of Minnesota.

What is the Midwest, and how do we best represent our region and terroir? Globalization opens the incredible opportunity to interact seamlessly with any corner of the world, the sharing of flavors and ideas inspiring so much growth. With that power, there is also a responsibility that is hard to articulate, but it's something we have ignored in the past. Looking inwards, in situ, what is authenticity? That is the driving force behind 3LECHE and (hopefully) articulated through the brands we produce and develop.

As we've changed, so has Naked Ballerina #2, now in version 3.0. This is what she looks like today:

3LECHE NAKED BALLERINA #2

- 20 ml Super Lemon
- 15 ml Paw-Paw Sweet Galium Nectar
- 45 ml Unum "Agave" Spirit

- 15 ml Allora Rosa Vermouth
- 2 dashes anisette bitters

Scale single serving recipe -> large format batch. Dilute to 14% ABV with Befuma Ispahan Hydrosol. Package (bottle or keg). Chill RTD cocktail before serving over ice.

The breakdown:

* Unum is our rail spirit line developed for bartenders, by bartenders. We source bulk spirits from large Midwest distilleries, co-packing the juice and not hiding the fact. Through our distributor partner, we can provide a wholesale price fit for menu placement, from dives to craft cocktails. We spend nothing on marketing and the design is very functional (read: inexpensive). What makes Unum special is that the proceeds go to Minnesota nonprofits with a predominant focus on the hospitality industry, and physical and mental health. We will have a distillery someday, but we have little interest in producing traditional spirits for distribution; Unum is our volume brand in the alcoholic market.

* Super Lemon and Paw-Paw Sweet Galium Nectar are under our Agrodulce label, a line of cocktail acids and syrups made from native and upcycled ingredients. Our partner Netzro works with us to collect spent citrus rinds from cocktail programs across the metro, and through their technology, they're able to create an end product that maintains the original character of the material without denaturing flavors. We use these to create a shelf-stable acid with a similar texture, pH, and flavor profile as freshly squeezed lemon juice. Paw-paw and sweet galium are native Minnesota raw plants that we use to emulate passion fruit and vanilla—it's delicious, and allows bartenders to express "tropicalia" without any agricultural products traditionally found closer to the equator.

* Allora is an aperitif and digestif company showcasing the terroir of the Midwest through locally grown and foraged botanicals. Old world heritage meets modern technique—our vision is to create an aperitivo hour in situ, mirroring the iconic Italian classics through the lens of this beautiful place we call home. Allora Rosa is made with a base of Minnesota-grown apple cider, which is surprisingly rare, it turns out—the majority of Midwest producers source cider apples from the coasts. Honeycrisp apples and the like make terrible cider—not enough tannins. We produce the cider in collaboration with our friends Milk & Honey Ciders in St. Joseph, Minnesota, founded by alumni of the horticulture program at the University of Minnesota, where the Forever Green Initiative is developing cold-hardy perennials that can survive our harsh winters. The cider is made from their apple #1734, the first true winter-hardy cider varietal by and for the Midwest.

* The final ingredient in the spec is anisette bitter. We make three styles of bitters which mirror the big boys: Angostura, Peychaud's, and Regan's Orange. Our anisette bitters highlights wild licorice in this (naturally dyed) amalgamation of native roots, barks, herbs, and flowers. This brand explains one of our value sets: we love Angostura/Campari, but what is the impact of bottling and shipping from Trinidad/Milan to the Twin Cities? Guests are used to an Old Fashioned or Negroni tasting a certain way, but is that enough of a reason to perpetuate supply chains in lieu of seeking more sustainable options? The bartender community is starting to discuss this more seriously. What is our moral and ethical responsibility when sourcing for our back bars? The counterpoint is the

Heinz argument. Heinz IS ketchup. Everything else is tomato sauce. It's pretentious, wrong, and expensive to think you can make something better than Heinz. I agree to a certain extent, but what if Heinz was open source, made everywhere, yet each region tasted slightly intriguingly different due to terroir? Could be a fun world.

If you live in Minnesota, you can access all the individual components to create the latest iteration of the Naked Ballerina #2. Build in tin, shake, strain, and serve. Or, you could just procure the completed cocktail in its ready-to-drink form, simply pour it over ice, and you're good. When packaging, instead of diluting the RTD with water to achieve the target ABV, we use a hydrosol of Befuma Ispahan. This idea for dilution was introduced to us by Empirical Spirits in Copenhagen. The result is flavor-on-flavor, and we think it's brilliant.

Befuma is a line of fermented botanical beverages, leveraging yeast and bacteria to produce delicious nonalcoholic tipples akin to kombucha. Ispahan's ferment starts with the Paw-Paw Sweet Galium Nectar as the yeast's food source; bacteria then consumes the resulting alcohol into a brilliantly delectable display of acids, or drinking vinegars. In addition to mirroring the sugar source in the cocktail, Befuma Ispahan also contains the same botanical structure as the Allora Rosa. We have five master botanical blends that show up in most of our unique product lines, differentiated by the base raw materials and technique applied, be it fermentation, maceration, or distillation. They are our mother sauces.

At the end of the day, the Naked Ballerina #2 is just a drink. I don't think this cocktail is particularly awe-inspiring or deserves to be in the canon of modern classics. I don't think the 3.0 version is perfect or finalized. I don't even think 3.0 is better than the original recipe, just different. It has been a muse that reflected an image of who I was in a moment and what I was thinking, continually inspiring the act of creation.

I'm curious to see what it looks like in another decade.

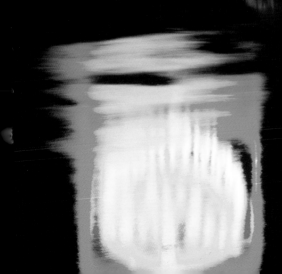

STOCKING YOUR MINNESOTA BAR

SUPPLIES

A properly stocked bar requires more than just a few glasses. Here's
what you'll need to become a home bartending pro.

Cocktail shaker	☐	Peeler	☐
Jigger	☐	Mixing glass	☐
Barspoon	☐	Corkscrew	☐
Cocktail strainer	☐	Glassware	☐
Fine-mesh strainer	☐	Pour spouts	☐
Muddler	☐	Blender	☐
Juicer	☐	Cocktail picks	☐

WHERE TO FIND THEM

The Twin Cities are filled with beautiful independent shops that stock
home bar essentials. Or, find what you need at Target, the Minneapolis-based company that's as much of a Minnesota institution as drinks
around a winter fire.

Cooks | Bellecour
cooksbellecour.com
Multiple locations

Umei
903 North Fifth Street
Minneapolis, MN 55401
shopumei.com

The Foundry Home Goods
110 5TH Avenue SE
Minneapolis, MN 55414
www.thefoundryhomegoods.com

Surdyk's
303 East Hennepin Avenue
Minneapolis, MN 55414
surdyks.com

Target
www.target.com

OTHER ESSENTIALS

Craftmade Aprons
Locally made chef and bartender aprons to keep your clothes clean—
and make you look like an expert.

Sota Clothing Backtrack Flask
To bring these well-crafted cocktails on the road.

Minnesota Ice
Blocks, pebbles, shaved—every style of ice made from pure, clear
Minnesota water.

Woah Nelly Spices
Minneapolis-made spice blends that can amp up any cocktail. (Pro tip:
try the smoked salt on the rim of a margarita.)

Well Told Glasses
Rocks and pint glasses with a map of the Twin Cities area to ensure
you're well-oriented even after a few drinks.

Earl Giles Disco Citrus
Perfect for fancy dried citrus garnishes.

THE SPIRITS

From booze to accompaniments, these locally made products are a must for any Twin Cities home bar.

3LECHE Botanical Refreshers
Canned N/A cocktails made from botanical blends.

Lovejoy's Bloody Mary Mix
An award-winning handmade, small-batch Bloody Mary mix made with all-natural ingredients.

Gray Duck Vodka
Paying homage to one of our proudest Minnesota quirks. (It's duck-duck-gray duck, not goose.)

Tattersall Aquavit
Perfect for adding a Nordic splash to drinks.

Red Locks Irish Whiskey
Minnesota-made with Irish expertise.

Brother Justus Cold-Peated Whiskey
New technique, familiar ingredients—all sourced from within 125 miles of the distillery.

Du Nord Gin
A juniper-forward blend of London dry and old-world gins.

Earl Giles Syrups and Elixirs
Classic flavors and unique combinations for your own craft cocktail menu.

Minneapple Apple Brandy
Made from local Honeycrisp apples—our fruity pride and joy.

Dashfire Bitters
An extensive collection of aromatic flavors inspired by global travels.

Dry Wit
Keep on hand to easily create mocktails for your spirit-free friends.

Tattersall Canned Cocktails
Pop them on ice at any outdoor social gathering during our precious Minnesota summers.

Grain Belt Premium and Hamm's Beer
No Minnesota bar is complete without these two classic, easy-drinking American-style lagers on hand, one that's brewed in Minneapolis, one that originated in St. Paul.

MINNEAPOLIS

ALL SAINTS
BILLY SUSHI / BILLY AFTER DARK
THE BRIAR
CAFÉ & BAR LURCAT
CENTRO
THE DAKOTA
FIKA
FRANCIS
HAI HAI
HEWING BAR & LOUNGE AND TULLIBEE RESTAURANT
LITTLE TIJUANA
LUSH LOUNGE & THEATER
MANNY'S STEAKHOUSE
MARA RESTAURANT & BAR
THE MARKET AT MALCOLM YARDS
MARTINA
NIGHTINGALE
OWAMNI
PALMER'S BAR
P.S. STEAK
RIVA TERRACE
SIDEBAR AT SURDYK'S
TERZO
VESTALIA HOSPITALITY:
BASEMENT BAR AT SOOKI & MIMI
THE BACK BAR AT YOUNG JONI
VOLSTEAD'S EMPORIUM

Any lifelong Minneapolitan will likely have a complicated relationship with what's been said about our city. "Flyover" rhetoric is tired and fusty, and it's been a long time since we've been having any of it. *Of course*, Minneapolis has got it all. Just ask the coastal transplants encroaching with increasingly rapid velocity.

Our city's (relative) livability—complete with the inexpensive cost of living, more shoreline than California, and it's regal status as hometown to Prince—is reflected in our bars and restaurants. All are mostly welcome, most places, most of the time, come as you are. Nothing is absolute, of course, and if you look for an outlier, you may find one. However, sophistication never steps into the lane of pretension, and our Midwestern work ethic and quirk means we take chances that don't necessarily follow trends.

Winter may deter some people, but when the snow is piling up shoulder high, give me a good old Minneapolis dive above anywhere else in the world. If you haven't shared the misery-loves-company, love-to-hate-it, unbridled joy/sorrow of a snowstorm over some brown liquor with your countrymen—well, you haven't lived.

For proof, belly up to one of our wonderful bars and test the limits of our "Minnesota Nice" with a bartender or some new friends. You're likely to come away with a newfound sense of what a city can be like when it stops getting stereotyped and is allowed to unfurl, frigid edges and all.

—Mecca Bos

ALL SAINTS

222 E HENNEPIN AVE, MINNEAPOLIS, MN 55414

With eight spirited cocktails and three to four spirit-free cocktails on a given night, Northeast Minneapolis restaurant All Saints is focused on quality over quantity when it comes to the beverage list. "Our cocktails are approachable, with roots in the classics and just enough nerdiness to keep things interesting," says bar manager Scott Weller. "We change about half of the menu seasonally, so there's always something new around the corner."

At All Saints—a delightfully buzzy restaurant that exudes understated glamour, chic comfort, and laid-back but detail-oriented service—the cocktails are also designed to pair loosely with the restaurant's wood-fired cuisine, which is focused on vegetables with a handful of meaty offerings. "Oftentimes this means sharing a common ingredient or complementary flavor between a drink and a dish," says Weller, pointing to The Gibby as an example. "The charred scallion vermouth pairs great with a bowl of our salt and pepper mushrooms with scallion dip-dip. I've always leaned on my love of cooking as inspiration for beverage development, which often means kitchen pantry ingredients and culinary techniques find their way into our drink-making process."

THE GIBBY

ALL SAINTS
222 E HENNEPIN AVE, MINNEAPOLIS, MN 55414

W e use a split base of vodka and gin and a dry vermouth steeped with charred scallions," says bar manager Scott Weller. "The addition of white balsamic, white pepper, and a pinch of salt also cranks up its savory qualities."

GLASSWARE: Stemmed cocktail glass
GARNISH: Skewered cocktail onion, sweety drop pepper

- 1 ¾ oz. vodka
- ¾ oz. London dry gin
- ½ oz. Charred Scallion Dry Vermouth (see recipe)

- 3 dashes Salt and Pepper Tincture (see recipe)
- 1 dash white balsamic vinegar

1. Stir all of the ingredients in a mixing glass filled with ice.

2. Strain the cocktail into a stemmed cocktail glass.

3. Garnish with a skewered cocktail onion and sweety drop pepper.

CHARRED SCALLION DRY VERMOUTH: Place 4 to 6 scallions (depending on size) onto an open-fire grill and leave them there until there is a heavy char. Put the charred scallions and a 750 ml bottle of Dolin Dry Vermouth into a container and let rest for up to 48 hours. Remove the scallions and run the vermouth through a cheesecloth or coffee filter to remove the remaining bits of char. Re-bottle the vermouth and store it in the refrigerator.

SALT AND PEPPER TINCTURE: Combine 1 tablespoon cracked white peppercorns, ½ teaspoon kosher salt, and 1 cup vodka. Let tincture sit for at least a few days before using. The flavors will get more pronounced over time, so taste periodically and strain off the peppercorns once it's at your desired level.

YOUNG BUCK (N/A)

ALL SAINTS
222 E HENNEPIN AVE., MINNEAPOLIS, MN 55414

According to Scott Weller, this cocktail is "a house-made ginger beer with a base of fresh ginger and carrot juice, brightened with sour orange and spiced with coriander and cinnamon."

GLASSWARE: Collins glass
GARNISH: Candied ginger

- Soda water, as needed
- ¾ oz. Sour Orange Juice (see recipe)

- 2 oz. Young Buck Mix (see recipe)

1. Fill a collins glass with ice.
2. Fill the glass three-quarters of the way to the top with soda water.
3. Add the Sour Orange Juice.
4. Add the Young Buck Mix over the top.

SOUR ORANGE JUICE: Add just enough hot water to 60 grams citric acid to dissolve the granules, then add 1 liter fresh orange juice.

YOUNG BUCK MIX: Combine 500 ml fresh ginger juice, 1 liter fresh carrot juice, 15 grams coriander, ¼ teaspoon cinnamon, and ½ teaspoon vitamin C powder. Blend the ingredients with an immersion blender for 30 seconds. Strain off the spices. Add simple syrup and whisk to blend.

BILLY SUSHI/BILLY AFTER DARK

116 N 1ST AVE., MINNEAPOLIS, MN 55401

Once you go Billy, you never go back.

Billy Tserenbat broke into the sushi scene way back in the early aughts in a semi-far-flung (yet very monied) suburb of Minneapolis called Wayzata, where the lake shores are blue, and the pockets are deep. Denizens of that wee but well-known 'burb made Sushi Fix their own personal playground, not just for the spot-on sushi, precise as a samurai's sword, but also for the sake and liquor that flowed like cash out of a hedge fund.

Infamously, the "shot-ski" became a way to prove your imbibing mettle. It's exactly what it sounds like—a number of shot glasses affixed to a ski. It means everyone in your party must down a shot at precisely the same time and velocity, unless one of you wants to be wearing Suntory down the front of your frock. While there's a certain frat (but fun) aspect to that particular maneuver, make no mistake about Sushi Fix's new sister location in downtown Minneapolis, Billy Sushi, and its secret speakeasy, Billy After Dark. That's where you'll find some of the finest—and most fun—Japanese whiskeys, and libations of all stripes, period.

"Everybody thinks that sushi is this elegant thing, but it can also be one of the most playful, depending on the sushi chef," Tserenbat explains of his philosophy, both on the plate and behind the bar. See a sushi roll designed to look like Santa's face at Christmastime, for instance, with what else but bluefin tuna for his red hat. But this is also the place to get the best and freshest fish—they turn over about 800 pounds of bluefin a week. That's *a lot* of little Santa hats.

And while Billy's places are known as stomping grounds for visiting celebrities and other bigwigs to let it all hang out, Tserenbat himself is a family man now, and so the speakeasy closes at 11:59 p.m.: "Because I have a midnight curfew, and nothing good happens after midnight."

If you want what *is* good, however, you'll have to go to know.

"It's a speakeasy, so that means I can't talk about it!" He doesn't want the whole world knowing about the place, preferring to let word spread by mouth. Even the Insta page is just a logo and a set of clues and rules, including "no phones," and the website redirects to a "free online money" page. Totally cheeky, totally funny, totally Billy.

His origin story, as he tells it, goes that he was born in Mongolia into a monied family, and then he moved to San Francisco and got cut off from his parents' generosity. "They told me to go and get a job."

Because the only job "experience" he had was eating sushi on his parents' dime, his friend's dad, who owned a sushi restaurant, took mercy on him and gave him a gig. It's the first and last gig he's ever had. "And now I'm known as the guy who does a pretty good job with sushi."

DON'T SWEAT THE TECHNIQUE

BILLY SUSHI/BILLY AFTER DARK
116 N 1ST AVE, MINNEAPOLIS, MN 55401

'90's hip-hop is king at Billy After Dark, and this anthem by Erik B. & Rakim is a well-known mic-dropper for anyone who knows and loves the genre. Cinnamon, tea, and brown liquor is worthy of the vibe.

GLASSWARE: Highball glass

GARNISH: Pebble ice dusted with cinnamon

- 1 ½ oz. Red Locks Irish Whiskey
- 1 oz. white peach
- ½ oz. simple syrup
- ½ oz. mizu green tea
- ½ oz. lemon juice

1. Combine all of the ingredients in a cocktail shaker with ice.

2. Shake.

3. Pour the cocktail into a highball.

4. Garnish with pebble ice dusted with cinnamon.

ALL EYEZ ON ME

BILLY SUSHI/BILLY AFTER DARK
116 N 1ST AVE., MINNEAPOLIS, MN 55401

A wine glass filled with effervescent cava and herbaceous accompaniments is sure to capture attention. A bold drink named after a song by the boldest of rappers. Tupac Shakur.

GLASSWARE: Wine glass

- 3 oz. Brut Cava
- 1 oz. Ferrand Cognac
- ½ oz. Bénédictine

- ½ oz. lemon juice
- ¼ oz. simple syrup

1. Shake all of the ingredients over ice.

2. Strain into a wine glass.

THE BRIAR

1231 WASHINGTON ST. NE, MINNEAPOLIS, MN 55413

Think of the perfect all-day neighborhood café: the best coffee program, a refined but approachable food menu, meticulous N/A cocktails, and a warm, European-vibes interior.

Congratulations, you've just willed The Briar into existence.

Opened in 2023, Briar is the brainchild of owners Abe Ziaimehr, Hilari Ziaimehr, and Evan Goldenrod, all veterans of the hospitality industry (Goldenrod tended bar at the legendary Marvel Bar, and Abe Ziaimehr cooked at Travail). The Briar feels like it's been an anchor in the Northeast Minneapolis community for decades. Bent cane chairs, intimate cocktail tables, beautifully made mortadella sandwiches on scratch focaccia, vinyl spinning on a turntable, and a space that flows openly between the bar and small open kitchen makes the Briar feel like a classic salon on the Left Bank of Paris in the 1920s. Add to it the lively conversation, clinking vintage China plates, and sunshine glinting from the large windows, and you have a neighborhood café where you can settle in all day and into the evening.

NATURAL K'EVAN (N/A)

THE BRIAR
1231 WASHINGTON ST. NE, MINNEAPOLIS, MN 55413

This booze-free concoction slides a delightfully earthy, northern flavor profile of pine and maple underneath the refreshment of tart pomegranate and citrus. Mugolio is pine-cone-bud syrup.

GLASSWARE: Rocks glass
GARNISH: Lemon peel coin

- 40 ml pomegranate juice
- 7 ml mugolio
- 2 ml All the Bitter New Orleans Bitters
- 2 ml maple syrup
- 2 ml saline solution
- Soda water, to top

1. Stir all of the ingredients, except for the soda water, over large ice.

2. Pour the cocktail into a rocks glass.

3. Top with soda water.

4. Serve with lemon peel coin, after expressing the lemon oils over the top.

TROPICALÍA (N/A)

THE BRIAR
1231 WASHINGTON ST. NE, MINNEAPOLIS, MN 55413

I't's all right there in the name—an alcohol-free, sunny refresher comprised of a floral hibiscus tea and a vinegary mango shrub.

GLASSWARE: Collins glass

GARNISH: Orange coin

- 120 ml Tropical Tea (see recipe)
- 25 ml Mango Shrub (see recipe)

1. Build the cocktail in a collins glass.

2. Garnish with an orange coin.

TROPICAL TEA
- 90 grams sencha tea
- 60 grams dried hibiscus flowers
- 15 grams licorice root
- 5,250 ml cold-filtered water

1. Combine all the dry ingredients in a large container. Add hot water (at least 185°F) to cover the tea and allow it to sit for 2 minutes.

2. Add the cold water and allow the tea to steep in the refrigerator for 15 hours.

3. Strain the tea through a fine-mesh chinois.

4. Refrigerate until ready to use.

Mango Shrub

- 1 case Ataulfo mangoes
- 1 liter sugar
- 750 ml Condimela Apple Balsamic Vinegar
- 400 ml kombucha vinegar
- 100 ml Champagne vinegar

1. Cut and peel the mangoes.
2. Add the sugar to the cut fruit and stir and mash a bit until incorporated.
3. Let the mixture sit for 15 to 24 hours.
4. Add the vinegars to the mango syrup. Stir well until the sugar is fully dissolved.
5. Let the shrub sit for at least 2 days.
6. Taste the shrub after 2 days to see if it has achieved the desired flavor.
7. Strain the shrub through a fine-mesh chinois twice into a large food container.
8. Refrigerate.

CAFÉ & BAR LURCAT

1624 HARMON PL., MINNEAPOLIS, MN 55403

Since 2002, Café Lurcat has served as an anchor to Loring Park. The elegant restaurant complements the lush, open green space with magnificent chandeliers, white tablecloths, tufted chairs, gourmet American cuisine, and a sunny patio with views of the Walker Art Center's sculpture garden.

Helmed by beverage director and sommelier Ross Kupitz and head bartender Ole Johnson, the cocktail list is rooted in respect for the traditional cocktail model: base spirit, modifier ingredient, citrus or sour, sugar, and a bitter component.

How would you characterize your approach to the Lurcat cocktail program?

Ross: Fresh ingredients and classic and unique flavor combinations. Beverages are also the ultimate "condiment" for our culinary team's food. The bar team is intimately involved in menu development, and is encouraged to experiment and push the program to be its best.

Ole: The bar staff likes to experiment and create recipes for syrups, infusions, and spirit-batched products that ultimately create new flavors as they meld together. A common sentiment for the bar team is, "Why buy when you can create?"

What sets the cocktail menu at Lurcat apart?

Ross: Balance. No one spirit dominates over the others on the menu, keeping a balance of base spirit flavor profiles for our guests. But more importantly, balance in each cocktail itself. A well-balanced cocktail will be delicious on its own, but will also enhance the dining experience by being food friendly.

Ole: Ross takes a team approach to cocktail creation, which creates a balance for the overall menu. Our collective travels fuel some of the inspiration, and each individual bartender brings a melting pot of ideas.

How does the cocktail menu accompany Café & Bar Lurcat's spectacular surroundings?

Ross: Timeless elegance. Richard D'Amico's vision has stood the test of time, from sun-drenched patio days with views of Loring Park to the stunning winter "snow globe" through our floor-to-ceiling windows. Our beverage program uses particular glassware for each cocktail that not only enhances the visual stimulation, but also allows the best aromas and flavors to shine. We serve our cocktails in the fashion of that timeless elegance.

What makes the Twin Cities cocktail scene special?

Ross: Camaraderie and knowledge. Healthy competition is always fun, but at its core, the beverage community around town is uplifting and supports continuing education for all who seek it. Another example of camaraderie is working with the great people at the import, supplier, and distribution levels. Building relationships and gaining more product knowledge through our vendors is another way we allow our team to create unique cocktails and expose our guests to new products.

PETIT JOLIE L'ORANGE

CAFÉ & BAR LURCAT
1624 HARMON PL., MINNEAPOLIS, MN 55403

This cocktail is Bar Lurcat's version of a gin Martini. It's spirit-forward, but well balanced.

GLASSWARE: Martini glass, chilled

GARNISH: Lemon peel

- 2 ½ oz. Lurcat's gin blend (50 percent Death's Door Gin, 50 percent London dry gin)
- 1 oz. Dolin Dry Vermouth
- 1 barspoon Italicus Bergamotto

1. Combine all of the ingredients in a mixing glass.
2. Add ice and stir to chill and dilute.
3. Strain the cocktail into a chilled martini glass.
4. Garnish with a lemon peel expressed over the finished product.

ESPRESSO MARTINI

CAFÉ & BAR LURCAT
1624 HARMON PL., MINNEAPOLIS, MN 55403

A precisely made version of the popular cocktail that allows the creamy flavors of vanilla and hazelnut to shine through the espresso.

GLASSWARE: Coupe glass, chilled

GARNISH: 3 roasted coffee beans, lemon peel

- 1 ½ oz. Stolichnaya Vanil Vodka
- 1 oz. Lavazza Espresso (a long-draw pour out of a single espresso pod)
- ½ oz. St. George NOLA Coffee Liqueur
- ½ oz. Frangelico

1. Combine all of the ingredients into a shaker tin with ice.

2. Shake vigorously to chill, dilute, and produce a slight crema.

3. Double-strain the cocktail through a fine-mesh strainer into a chilled coupe glass.

4. Garnish with three roasted coffee beans and a lemon peel expressed over the finish product.

CENTRO

1414 QUINCY ST. NE, MINNEAPOLIS, MN 55413

With crushable tacos, classic Mexican-inspired cocktails, and a bright, colorful setting, this perpetually packed fast-casual spot hits all the right notes. At all three locations of the popular Mexican restaurant—Northeast Minneapolis, Eat Street, and the Highland Park neighborhood of St. Paul—the cocktail menu focuses on handcrafted agave-centric drinks, with many of the classics scaled to offer on tap—the perfect approach for a lively, energetic restaurant.

QUINCY MARGARITA

CENTRO
1414 QUINCY ST. NE, MINNEAPOLIS, MN 55413

Centro's take on the classic Margarita gets the orange flavor from locally made Tattersall Orange Crema.

GLASSWARE: Rocks glass

GARNISH: Lime slice

- Salt, for the rim
- 2 oz. tequila
- 1 oz. lime juice

- ½ oz. simple syrup
- ½ oz. Tattersall Orange Crema

1. Salt the rim of a rocks glass.

2. Combine all of the ingredients in a cocktail shaker.

3. Shake.

4. Pour the cocktail into the salted glass and garnish with a lime slice.

MORELOS SOUR

CENTRO

1414 QUINCY ST. NE, MINNEAPOLIS, MN 55413

The perfect combination of mellow heat, a touch of sweet, a little earthiness, and a puckery-sour flavor make this an expertly balanced cocktail.

GLASSWARE: Rocks glass

GARNISH: Lime slice

- Agave worm salt, for the rim
- 2 oz. bourbon
- ¾ oz. chipotle sour
- ¾ oz. simple syrup
- ½ oz. lemon juice

1. Salt the rim of a rocks glass with agave worm salt.

2. Combine all of the ingredients in a cocktail shaker.

3. Shake.

4. Pour the cocktail into the salted glass and garnish with a lime slice.

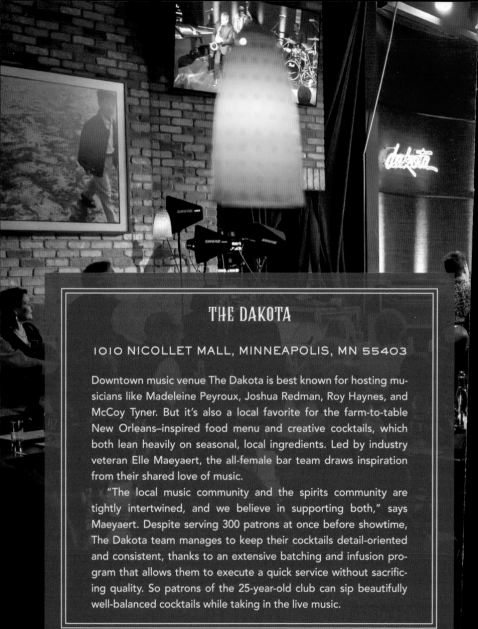

THE DAKOTA

1010 NICOLLET MALL, MINNEAPOLIS, MN 55403

Downtown music venue The Dakota is best known for hosting musicians like Madeleine Peyroux, Joshua Redman, Roy Haynes, and McCoy Tyner. But it's also a local favorite for the farm-to-table New Orleans–inspired food menu and creative cocktails, which both lean heavily on seasonal, local ingredients. Led by industry veteran Elle Maeyaert, the all-female bar team draws inspiration from their shared love of music.

"The local music community and the spirits community are tightly intertwined, and we believe in supporting both," says Maeyaert. Despite serving 300 patrons at once before showtime, The Dakota team manages to keep their cocktails detail-oriented and consistent, thanks to an extensive batching and infusion program that allows them to execute a quick service without sacrificing quality. So patrons of the 25-year-old club can sip beautifully well-balanced cocktails while taking in the live music.

MR. SMOOTH

THE DAKOTA
1010 NICOLLET MALL, MINNEAPOLIS, MN 55403

The Mr. Smooth was named for Irv Williams, an American jazz legend and lifelong Twin Cities resident, and was designed to capture the complexity and strength of its legendary namesake. This is the version that Irv himself approved before his passing at 100 years of age.

GLASSWARE: Coupe glass

GARNISH: Orange peel

- 2 oz. bourbon
- ¼ oz. cognac
- ¼ oz. Cynar
- ¼ oz. demerara simple syrup
- 2 dashes Angostura bitters

1. Add all of the ingredients to a cocktail shaker over ice.

2. Stir thoroughly.

3. Strain the cocktail into a coupe glass.

4. Garnish with an orange peel.

BOURBON STREET SMASH

THE DAKOTA
IOIO NICOLLET MALL, MINNEAPOLIS, MN 55403

This drink honors the city that inspires The Dakota's food and much of the music lineup: New Orleans. It takes a traditional Bourbon Smash and adds locally sourced ingredients, such as rhubarb and maple leaf tea, encompassing all of what makes The Dakota special.

GLASSWARE: Collins glass
GARNISH: Fresh mint leaves

- 2 oz. bourbon
- 1 ½ oz. Rhubarb and Maple Leaf Tea Syrup (see recipe)
- 2 oz. Brown Sugar Sour (see recipe)
- Mint leaves, as needed

1. Combine the bourbon, tea syrup, and sour in a shaker over ice.
2. Add a few leaves of mint.
3. Shake hard.
4. Pour the cocktail and ice into a collins glass.
5. Garnish with fresh mint.

RHUBARB AND MAPLE LEAF TEA SYRUP: Grind 12 dehydrated maple leaves into small flakes. Simmer with 4 cups sugar, 6 cups water, and 3 cups chopped rhubarb. Simmer the mixture until the rhubarb is mushy and falling apart, at least 30 minutes. Strain it through a fine-mesh strainer. (You can substitute Earl Grey tea for the maple leaves; use three tea bags.)

BROWN SUGAR SOUR: In a saucepan, combine 2 cups turbinado sugar, ¼ teaspoon kosher salt, and 2 cups water. Heat the mixture and stir until the sugars and salt are dissolved. Take 2 cups of the resulting syrup and combine it with 1 cup lemon juice and 1 cup lime juice.

FIKA

2600 PARK AVE., MINNEAPOLIS, MN 55407

In Swedish, the word *fika* means time to sit with friends, family, and colleagues to eat, drink, and connect. Fortunately, the American Swedish Institute (ASI) provides a place to do just that: an on-site café aptly named FIKA. The bright, sunny space features coffee, baked goods, breakfast, lunch, and cocktails that highlight Swedish culinary flavors and traditions. Take in an aquavit cocktail, then roam the ASI to learn about the history and contemporary culture of one of Minnesota's most significant immigrant populations.

WHITE WINE GLÖGG

FIKA

2600 PARK AVE., MINNEAPOLIS, MN 55407

T his is ASI president/CEO Bruce Karstadt's personal recipe for *glögg*, a Swedish mulled wine. FIKA serves this drink every holiday season.

GLASSWARE: Mug

GARNISH: Raisins, blanched almonds

- 12 whole cloves
- 6 whole cardamom pods
- 2 star anise
- 1 (750 ml) bottle sweet white wine
- ½ cup fine sugar

- 1 long strip orange peel
- 1 cinnamon stick
- 1 piece of fresh, peeled ginger, approximately 1 inch
- 4 oz. orange-flavored vodka or cognac (optional)

1. Toast and crush the cloves, cardamom, and star anise and place them in a tea bag or spice bag.

2. Mix the wine, sugar, spice bag, orange peel, cinnamon stick, and ginger together.

3. Heat the mixture in a saucepan over medium heat. Simmer for 5 minutes.

4. Remove the pan from heat. Cover it and leave it to stand for an hour.

5. Strain off the spices.

6. For a stronger version, add vodka or cognac after cooking.

7. Serve with a spoonful of raisins—golden or regular—and slivered almonds in each cup.

AQUAVIT SIDECAR

FIKA
2600 PARK AVE., MINNEAPOLIS, MN 55407

This recipe comes courtesy of ASI's Nordic Table instructor Patrice Johnson, who included this recipe in her book *Jul: Swedish American Holiday Traditions* (Minnesota Historical Society Press).

GLASSWARE: Coupe glass

GARNISH: Orange peel

- 2 oz. Gamle Ode Dill-Flavored Aquavit
- ¾ oz. fresh-squeezed lemon juice
- ¾ oz. Tattersall Orange Crema

1. Pour the liquids into a shaker filled with ice.

2. Shake well.

3. Strain the cocktail into a coupe.

4. Garnish with an orange peel.

FRANCIS

2422 CENTRAL AVE. NE, MINNEAPOLIS, MN 55418

Francis, in Northeast Minneapolis, gets its name and ethos from the tale of Francis the pig, a legendary porcine hero who escaped slaughter in Canada, and was memorialized in song by Canadian punk band Propagandhi. This fully vegan restaurant serves a menu of burgers, chili fries, and other late-night greasy eats, all completely free of animal anything and yet just as delicious (if not more so) as many of the restaurant's flesh-focused peers. The bar program, crafted by Nick Kosevich, features vegan cocktails that similarly push expectations of what you'd find at a vegan restaurant.

SCHRUTES AND LADDERS

FRANCIS
2422 CENTRAL AVE. NE, MINNEAPOLIS, MN 55418

The Schrutes and Ladders is a clever homage to beet farmer, paper seller, and favorite son of Scranton, Dwight Schrute, featuring an earthy beet base and herbal notes of aquavit.

GLASSWARE: Large coupe glass

GARNISH: Pickles of your choice

- 2 oz. Gamle Ode Celebration Aquavit
- 2 oz. Midwest Juicery Beet and Carrot
- 1 ½ oz. Earl Giles Grapefruit Lime Elixir
- ¼ barspoon methylcellulose

1. Combine all of the ingredients in a shaker over ice and double-shake.

2. Strain the cocktail into a large coupe glass.

3. Garnish with pickles.

HAI HAI

2121 UNIVERSITY AVE. NE, MINNEAPOLIS, MN 55418

When she started her food truck, Hola Arepa, Christina Nguyen's food stylings were a welcome and refreshing addition to the Twin Cities food scene. Hola, as those in the know simply call it, is as much respite as it is restaurant: its hip, cool Caribbean vibes can warm even the coldest Minnesotan on the most frigid of days. Their mango-, mezcal-, rum-, and horchata-laced cocktails have a lot do with it.

But as much as we crush on Hola, its sister restaurant, HAI HAI, just might be its cuter little sibling. Housed in a now-shuttered, infamously lowbrow yet beloved strip club called The Deuce Deuce in Northeast Minneapolis, (*hai hai* roughly translates to the same thing in Vietnamese) the restaurant and bar is one of the prettiest in town. Floral table liners, lush foliage, banana leaf lined plates, and swoon-worthy rattan chandeliers set a tropical scene for food and drinks inspired both by Nguyen's roots as a Vietnamese American, as well as her travels.

Though she had always had a Vietnamese spot kicking around her creative imagination, she wasn't sure if she had anything to add. Minneapolis is home to a large Vietnamese immigrant community, and its resultant restaurant scene means we think of pho and bánh mi as straight-up Minnesota cooking. Still, when she started traveling the entirety of Southeast Asia, Nguyen realized that there were still many flavors of the region unfamiliar to the greater Minnesota palate, and she would bring them to Minnesotans.

The bar program infuses fun Southeast Asian flavors into classics, and takes the sweet edge off of beloved tropical drinks to make them feel a bit more adult. Fresh sugarcane juice provides a backbone for many HAI HAI libations, inducing a simple sugarcane juice plus ginger

Juicing sugarcane

lime plus Thai basil plus choose-your-own-spirit that makes up the house drink, Next Up. Infusing ingredients like pennywort, fermented rice, and Vietnamese cinnamon keeps imbibers at HAI HAI constantly in a state of discovery.

"Vacation is a state of mind," says Nguyen, "We're trying to transport people to Southeast Asia, where there are big, luscious, beautiful plants, and a feeling of warmth—not always easy to create in a Minnesota winter."

Pro tip: HAI HAI has an indoor/outdoor patio that opens as long as the temps rise above 25°F. Also, there's "maybe a hidden stripper pole" on the premises—a relic from the place's more red-light pedigree.

NEXT UP . . .

HAI HAI
2121 UNIVERSITY AVE. NE, MINNEAPOLIS, MN 55418

This drink was inspired by travels through Southeast Asia, where you can get fresh sugarcane juice on the street anywhere you go. It's great with any spirit, and the name is a nod to the former business, as in, "Next up (to the stage). . . ." You can use any spirit you like in place of the rum. If you can't get fresh sugarcane juice, you can substitute canned sugarcane juice, which can be found at most Asian grocery stores.

GLASSWARE: Collins glass
GARNISH: Thai basil bouquet, dehydrated ginger

- 2 ½ oz. freshly pressed sugarcane juice
- 2 oz. rum
- ½ oz. Ginger Syrup (see recipe)
- ½ oz. fresh lime juice

1. Combine all of the ingredients in a cocktail shaker with ice.

2. Shake vigorously.

3. Strain the cocktail into a collins glass with ice.

4. Garnish with a Thai basil bouquet and a piece of dehydrated ginger.

GINGER SYRUP: Peel and rough-chop enough ginger to yield 1 cup of juice. Run the ginger through a juice extractor. Take the discarded pulp from the juice extractor, wrap it in cheesecloth, and press it in a basket strainer. Prep 1 cup ginger juice this way, then mix it with 1 cup simple syrup and a pinch of salt.

POSTCARDS FROM PALAWAN

HAI HAI
2121 UNIVERSITY AVE. NE, MINNEAPOLIS, MN 55418

A play on a spicy Margarita, this drink uses real tamarind for an earthy, tart flavor, plus pineapple to balance its acidity and spice from the Thai chile.

GLASSWARE: Rocks glass
GARNISH: Thin pineapple round and fronds

- 2 oz. Tamarind and Thai Chile–Infused Mezcal (see recipe)
- 1 oz. pineapple juice
- ¾ oz. simple syrup
- ¾ oz. fresh lime juice

1. Combine all of the ingredients in a cocktail shaker with ice.

2. Shake vigorously.

3. Pour the cocktail into a rocks glass over ice.

4. Garnish with a thin pineapple round and fronds.

TAMARIND AND THAI CHILE–INFUSED MEZCAL: Combine 1 (750 ml) bottle La Luna Mezcal with 4 rough-chopped Thai chiles, ½ pineapple, rind removed and chopped, and 6 tamarind pods, shells removed. Steep for 24 to 48 hours. After steeping, strain the infusion through a basket strainer.

HEWING BAR & LOUNGE AND TULLIBEE RESTAURANT

300 N WASHINGTON AVE., MINNEAPOLIS, MN 55401

With a sauna, a year-round rooftop pool and hot tub, a collection of Minnesota-made products, and the Nordic-inspired menu at Tullibee restaurant, The Hewing Hotel takes inspiration from the state's Scandinavian roots while centering local makers and producers. Whether at Tullibee, in the rustic lobby bar, or on the rooftop, the Hewing's cocktail menus feature a range of locally made spirits, which are whipped into well-crafted drinks along with hyper-local ingredients, giving guests a taste of Minnesota.

HEWING OLD FASHIONED

**HEWING BAR & LOUNGE AND TULLIBEE RESTAURANT
300 N WASHINGTON AVE., MINNEAPOLIS, MN 55401**

GLASSWARE: Rocks glass
GARNISH: Orange peel

- 1 ½ oz. Knob Creek Hewing Private Barrel Bourbon
- ½ oz. Knob Creek Rye
- 2 dashes Bittercube Trinity Bitters
- ¼ oz. simple syrup

1. Add all of the ingredients together in a beaker or tumbler.
2. Stir.
3. Strain the cocktail into a rocks glass over a large ice cube.
4. Garnish with an orange peel.

HONEY BADGER

HEWING BAR & LOUNGE AND TULLIBEE RESTAURANT
300 N WASHINGTON AVE., MINNEAPOLIS, MN 55401

GLASSWARE: Nick & Nora glass

- 1 ½ oz. Old Forester Hewing Private Barrel Bourbon
- ¾ oz. Yellow Chartreuse
- ½ oz. honey
- ½ oz. Ginger Syrup (see recipe)
- ¼ oz. lime juice

1. Combine all of the ingredients in a cocktail shaker.

2. Shake.

3. Strain the cocktail into a Nick & Nora glass.

GINGER SYRUP: Bring ¾ cup water to a boil. Add 1 cup granulated sugar. Once the sugar is dissolved, add 1 cup peeled, sliced ginger root. Remove the mixture from heat and allow it to cool and steep in a covered pan for 1 hour. Strain the ginger out and use.

LITTLE TIJUANA

17 E 26TH ST., MINNEAPOLIS, MN 55408

Plenty of people are thoroughly confused when they visit Little Tijuana and discover that it's not a Mexican joint. Yet you can certainly order and enjoy one of the best Margaritas in town while you dig into a broad swath of internationally inflected dishes from the food menu, like potato pelmeni, papri chaat, or a perfectly pitched steam burger. In a word, Little T's is fun. Their motto? "Come in, stay a while, and don't be an asshole."

For decades, Little T's was a beloved late-night hang for massive platters of nachos to soak up the night's revelry, until it closed during the pandemic. The space was snapped up and given new life by a squadron of some of the most talented hospitality gentlemen in town: bartenders Bennett Johnson and Travis Serbus, Dan Manosack in the kitchen, and Ben Siers-Rients running ops. They kept the name, DIY-ed the interior, and re-opened the space as one of the best and least-pretentious cocktail spots around. The drink menu is streamlined, playful-yet-serious, and affordable. Little T's has quickly become the kind of spot where hospitality folks congregate after shifts, which is how you know it's something special.

SAZERAC THING

LITTLE TIJUANA
17 E 26TH ST., MINNEAPOLIS, MN 55408

Little T's takes the New Orleans classic and leans hard into earthy and herbal elements like aquavit, mole bitters and epazote syrup for a rendition that surprises and delights.

GLASSWARE: Rocks glass

GARNISH: Expressed lemon peel, atomized Pernod

- • 2 oz. Ida Graves Aquavit
- • ½ oz. epazote simple syrup
- • 4 dashes Peychaud's bitters
- • 3 dashes mole bitters

1. Build the drink in a mixing glass.

2. Add ice and stir until the mixture is properly chilled and diluted.

3. Pour the cocktail into a rocks glass over large format ice.

4. Express a lemon peel over the drink then drop the peel in, and spritz with atomized Pernod.

PIÑA COLADA

LITTLE TIJUANA
17 E 26TH ST., MINNEAPOLIS, MN 55408

This is the more well-traveled cousin of the beachside Piña Colada that never left the beachside party at the resort in Mexico, but is no less fun—the Cynar topper trick it picked up in Italy is the perfect foil to its vacation-familiar, coconutty sweetness.

GLASSWARE: Hurricane glass
GARNISH: Dehydrated lime wheel

- 2 oz. Ten To One Caribbean Rum
- 1 oz. Coco López Coconut Cream
- 1 oz. pineapple juice
- ¾ oz. lime juice
- 1 cup ice
- 1 oz. Cynar, to top

1. Add all of the ingredients, except for the Cynar, to a blender and blend until the ice is fully broken down and the drink has achieved a smooth, creamy consistency.

2. Pour the cocktail into a hurricane glass.

3. Garnish with a dehydrated lime wheel and straw.

4. Slowly pour the Cynar on the top.

LUSH LOUNGE & THEATER

990 CENTRAL AVE. NE, MINNEAPOLIS, MN 55413

With bright colors, poppy artwork, and a calendar of drag shows, burlesque performances, cabaret singers, bingo, gay-mes, and more, LUSH Lounge & Theater is all about love, inclusivity, personal expression, and fun. The cocktail menu features elevated classics with a twist, mixing the familiar with something unexpected to create absolute joy—just like a good drag show.

ESPRESSO MARTINI

LUSH LOUNGE & THEATER
990 CENTRAL AVE. NE, MINNEAPOLIS, MN 55413

Sweet and flavorful with a punch, it's just what you need to keep up on Lush's late-night dance floor.

GLASSWARE: Martini glass, chilled

GARNISH: Coffee beans

- 1 ¼ oz. Absolut Vanilia
- 1 ¼ oz. Three Olives Espresso
- 1 ¼ oz. hazelnut-infused cold press coffee

1. Combine all of the ingredients in a cocktail shaker.

2. Shake.

3. Pour the cocktail into a chilled martini glass.

4. Garnish with a few coffee beans.

LUSH 75

LUSH LOUNGE & THEATER
990 CENTRAL AVE. NE, MINNEAPOLIS, MN 55413

A bright, refreshing version of the classic French 75, perfect for imbibing on the bar's oasis-like patio, decked with trees and little white lights.

GLASSWARE: Highball glass

GARNISH: Lemon wedge

- 1 oz. Absolut Citron
- ½ oz. Tattersall Crème de Fleur
- ¼ oz. triple sec
- ¼ oz. simple syrup
- Champagne float

1. Combine all of the ingredients, except for the Champagne, in a highball over ice.

2. Stir.

3. Float the Champagne over the top.

4. Garnish with a lemon wedge.

MANNY'S STEAKHOUSE

825 S MARQUETTE AVE., MINNEAPOLIS, MN 55402

Everything at Manny's Steakhouse is obscenely large, over-the-top, and eye-popping—including the bill. Manny's has been the expense-account destination in downtown Minneapolis for decades, and their famous three-pound "Bludgeon of Beef" tomahawk steak needs an equally strong beverage to stand up to its might. There's nothing subtle here; upon entry, guests are greeted by a hulking portrait of a bull on the wall, flagrantly displaying its testicular fortitude in a not-so-subtle shotgun blast of testosterone to the face. It's beef and bourbon, folks. No need to complicate matters.

MANNY'S OLD FASHIONED

MANNY'S STEAKHOUSE
825 S MARQUETTE AVE., MINNEAPOLIS, MN 55402

There's no better place to have this classic cocktail, which uses locally made Red Locks Irish Whiskey and tops with a delicious Filthy Black Cherry (wild Italian Amarena cherries from Filthy, a Miami-based company that makes high-end mixology ingredients).

GLASSWARE: Martini glass
GARNISH: Expressed orange peel, Filthy Black Cherry

- **3 oz. Red Locks Irish Whiskey**
- **1 ½ oz. demerara syrup**
- **3 dashes Angostura bitters**
- **3 dashes Angostura orange bitters**

1. Combine all of the ingredients in a shaker and stir for 30 seconds.

2. Pour the cocktail over fresh ice into a rocks glass.

3. Garnish with an expressed orange peel and a black cherry from Filthy.

MANNY'S MANHATTAN

MANNY'S STEAKHOUSE
825 S MARQUETTE AVE., MINNEAPOLIS, MN 55402

With Minnesota-made Roknar Rye and Duluth-made Vikre Amaro, Manny's version puts a decidedly local spin on a classic. If you can't find Filthy Black Cherries in your area, you can use any high-end Amarena cherries.

GLASSWARE: Martini glass
GARNISH: Filthy Black Cherry

- 3 oz. Far North Roknar Rye
- 1 oz. Foro Sweet Vermouth
- ½ oz. Vikre Amaro

1. In a shaker with ice, combine all of the ingredients.

2. Stir for 30 seconds.

3. Strain the cocktail into a martini glass.

4. Drop in a Filthy Black Cherry for garnish.

MARA RESTAURANT & BAR

245 HENNEPIN AVE., MINNEAPOLIS, MN 55401

Mara—the buzzy, beautiful restaurant and bar at Four Seasons Hotel Minneapolis—not only attracts notable locals and visitors on the restaurant floor, but behind the scenes, too. Upon opening, the hotel nabbed some of the biggest culinary stars in the city, including chef/partner Gavin Kaysen, who along with his team has created a program that exudes next-level quality, stunning simplicity, well-executed balance, and artful presentation.

While the cocktails are excellently enjoyed in the bright, high-ceilinged, well-appointed restaurant, they somehow taste even better when sipped in the moody bar area, complete with plush booths, dim lighting, access to the gourmet food menu, and the occasional celebrity sighting.

ARPEGE

MARA RESTAURANT & BAR
245 HENNEPIN AVE., MINNEAPOLIS, MN 55401

This crisp cocktail is made with locally crafted Du Nord gin, and features light and layered floral notes and citrus flavors courtesy of 3LECHE's grapefruit rhubarb fermented botanical beverage.

GLASSWARE: Collins glass
GARNISH: Baby's breath, metal straw

- 75 ml seltzer
- 50 ml 3LECHE Pompelmo Fermented Botanical Beverage
- 20 ml verjus
- 20 ml bitter almond ratafia
- 15 ml vodka
- 15 ml Du Nord Prominence Gin
- 10 ml lemongrass-rose syrup
- 3 drops orange blossom water
- 2 drops citric and malic acid solution

1. Combine all of the ingredients in a collins glass over ice shards.

2. Garnish with baby's breath and add a metal straw.

MADHAUS

MARA RESTAURANT & BAR
245 HENNEPIN AVE., MINNEAPOLIS, MN 55401

I somalt, a sugar substitute, adds a note of sweetness to this slightly bitter, herbaceous drink.

GLASSWARE: Luigi Bormioli water glass
GARNISH: Isomalt Disc (see recipe), short metal straw

- 40 ml Earl Grey or anise hyssop tea
- 20 ml 3LECHE Aronia Acid
- 20 ml simple syrup
- 20 ml berry ratafia
- 15 ml gin

1. Combine all of the ingredients in a large water glass.

2. Add pebble ice.

3. Garnish with an Isomalt Disc.

ISOMALT DISC: Preheat the oven to 465°F. Put 18 to 20 grams isomalt in silicone tray molds. Place in the oven until the isomalt has melted and is translucent with air pockets. Remove the molds from the oven and add flower petals or herbs to the discs as they cool down. Once the isomalt discs are hard and cooled, remove them from the molds and store them in a dry container with silica packets.

THE MARKET AT MALCOLM YARDS

501 30TH AVE. SE, MINNEAPOLIS, MN 55414

Malcolm Yards isn't the first food hall–style establishment in the Twin Cities, but it's the first with a serious bar program. Opened in 2021 in the historic Harris Machinery Building in an old trainyard—right between Surly Brewing and O'Shaughnessy Distillery—the structure is all weathered limestone, rusty steel beams, and preserved graffiti from its (many) years as an abandoned playground for mischievous youths. Nine modern kitchen stalls host a rotating stable of local food businesses of dizzying variety, there's a self-pour tap wall, and the drink menu is legit, coming from the mind of local legend Nick Kosevich.

ARGENTINE SOUR

THE MARKET AT MALCOLM YARDS
501 30TH AVE. SE, MINNEAPOLIS, MN 55414

There is no place on earth that loves Fernet more than Argentina," says Nick. "Seventy-five percent of the entire production of Fernet is consumed in Argentina. This cocktail is a nod to that phenomenon, as well as some other flavors from Argentina: maté, guava, and prickly pear."

GLASSWARE: Coupe glass
GARNISH: Lime wheel, 2 spritzes of guava essence and tiger viola

- 2 oz. Earl Giles Grapefruit-Lime Elixir
- 2 oz. water
- 1 oz. maté
- 1 oz. Earl Giles Vodka
- 1 oz. fernet
- ½ oz. singani

1. Combine all of the ingredients over ice and chill.

2. Pour the cocktail into a coupe glass.

3. Garnish with a lime wheel and two spritzes of guava essence and tiger viola.

THE NORTHERN WAY

THE MARKET AT MALCOLM YARDS
501 30TH AVE. SE, MINNEAPOLIS, MN 55414

 Collins-style cocktail using northern flavors.

GLASSWARE: Collins glass

GARNISH: Charred rosemary sprig

- **2 oz. ginger lemon honey elixir**
- **2 oz. vodka**
- **2 oz. water**
- **2 dashes Bittercube Blackstrap Bitters**

1. Combine all of the ingredients in a mixing glass.

2. Pour the cocktail into a collins glass over good ice.

3. Garnish by inserting the charred rosemary sprig in the glass.

MARTINA

4312 UPTON AVE. S, MINNEAPOLIS, MN 55410

Martina exploded onto the scene in 2017 on a quiet corner of the charming south Minneapolis neighborhood of Linden Hills, and has since been a must-stop destination for anyone interested in the Twin Cities cocktail scene. The bar program, originally started by Marco Zappia (now of 3LECHE), uses only house-made botanicals, ferments, and blended, non-branded spirits. Now led by longtime bar manager Adam Luesse (pictured at right), the drinks at Martina continue to build on a legacy of inventive playfulness, as cocktails often come garnished with feathers or elaborately carved limes. The cocktails dance around Italian digestivo/aperitivo culture, perfectly complementing chef Danny del Prado's bold Argentinian/Italian cuisine.

BONAPERA

MARTINA
4312 UPTON AVE. S, MINNEAPOLIS, MN 55410

Typical of the drinks and food at Martina, the Bonapera layers complex flavor elements into something that ends up feeling seamless, smooth, and elemental.

GLASSWARE: Lowball glass

- 20 ml Americano vermouth
- 15 ml macerated brandy/ grappa blend
- 15 ml yerba maté iced tea
- 5 ml rye whiskey

- 5 ml St. George Spiced Pear Liqueur
- 5 ml demerara syrup
- 2 eye droppers Angostura bitters

1. Combine all of the ingredients in a cocktail shaker.

2. Lightly stir.

3. Serve the cocktail over ice in a lowball glass.

NIGHTINGALE

2551 LYNDALE AVE. S, MINNEAPOLIS, MN 55405

In the increasingly gentrified Uptown neighborhood, a geography that was once rife with indie bars, restaurants, record stores, salons, and coffee shops but is now more corporate than not, Nightingale remains.

Carrie McCabe-Johnston and Jasha Johnston make a dream team. Partners in both business and life, Carrie holds down the kitchen while Jasha makes the bar one of the best in town. Since opening a decade ago, they've added several more bars to their hospitality group, mostly beloved, down-market neighborhood watering holes. But instead of scooping them up and gentrifying them beyond all recognition, they simply give these spots a loving spit shine and the ongoing daily TLC that a classic warhorse of a place deserves.

But Nightingale is their baby, a family-owned gem, the place everyone wishes they had right around the corner. Well-worn leather stools, cozy banquettes, a DJ on the weekends, and staff who know your name. And that's before mentioning the food and drink.

This is an industry bar—you know the type—where cooks, chefs, and bartenders head after hanging up their aprons for a $3 Hamm's, a spot-on Sazerac, and anything in between. It's one of the few remaining late-night places to eat in Uptown; the kitchen stays open until midnight every night, and the prices stay affordable—no $18 Old Fashioneds here.

And, if you're in the mood for a slightly more downscale vibe, no fear. The Johnstons' loving hands have scooped up the excellent and indefatigable Dusty's Northeast, known for its dubiously named Dago, basically a cheeseburger but with pork and red sauce; Liquor Lyle's, which will become a pinball bar when all is said and done; and Mortimer's, the very spot where Jasha cut his young teeth under the tutelage of Carrie's dad, who used to run the place.

Thanks to this couple, these cherished haunts have narrowly missed the wrecking ball and will instead stay populated with drinkers for years, and probably decades to come.

GOD SAVE THE QUEEN

NIGHTINGALE
2551 LYNDALE AVE. S, MINNEAPOLIS, MN 55405

I f there's any queen worthy of saving, it's the honeybee. Her fruits are utilized elagantly with this cocktail.

GLASSWARE: Nick & Nora glass

GARNISH: Micro lavender, absinthe spritz

- 1 ½ oz. J. Carver Barrel Aged Gin
- ¾ oz. Cocchi Americano Bianco
- ½ oz. Bee Pollen-Honey Syrup (see recipe)
- ¼ oz. lemon juice

1. Combine all of the ingredients in a shaker.

2. Shake.

3. Pour the cocktail into a Nick & Nora glass over ice.

4. Garnish with a very small sprig of lavender and a spritz of atomized absinthe.

BEE POLLEN-HONEY SYRUP: Combine 1 cup boiling water and ⅓ cup bee pollen. Stir until both are dissolved. Use whatever leftover syrup you have drizzled over vanilla ice cream.

CHUPACABRA

NIGHTINGALE

2551 LYNDALE AVE. S, MINNEAPOLIS, MN 55405

The chupacabra is the infamous creature that haunts countries all over the Americas. This drink packs a venomous bite worthy of its namesake with tequila, pepper, and tomatillo. This recipe comes from Jakob McCabe-Johnston.

GLASSWARE: Rocks glass

GARNISH: Fresh-cracked pepper

- **Pink Himalayan salt, for the rim**
- **2 parts reposado tequila**
- **1 part Roasted Tomatillo Syrup (see recipe)**

1. Rim a rocks glass with pink Himalayan salt. Combine ingredients in a cocktail tin.

2. Shake vigorously.

3. Pour the cocktail into the rocks glass over ice.

4. Garnish with fresh-cracked pepper.

ROASTED TOMATILLO SYRUP: Roast or grill ¼ lb. tomatillos until they are charred in spots and softened. Meanwhile, boil ¾ cup water with ¼ cup plus 2 tablespoons agave syrup. Let both components cool. Blend the charred tomatillos, agave syrup, and a serrano chile pepper together, then strain. Add 1 cup lime juice.

OWAMNI

420 S IST ST., MINNEAPOLIS, MN 55401

Go to Owmani, Minneapolis' first Native American–owned-and-operated restaurant—and one of the few in the country—and you'll soon understand that nothing is done without intention here.

That is, if you can get in. Booked solid since the day they opened in 2021, the restaurant overlooking the falls of the Mississippi River—once a sacred place for the Dakota people called *Owámniyomni*, or "the place of the falling swirling waters" in Dakota—might be the country's most notoriously difficult reservation to get.

When people recognize owner and chef Sean Sherman, the first thing they ask is usually, "How do I get in?" Pro tip: walk in and sit at the bar. It's easy to see, hear, smell, and taste what all the fuss is about. A playlist composed of all Native American musicians—Redbone, Jimi Hendrix, powwow songs—sets the tone not just for dinner, but for an experience.

The neon red signage at the doorframe, reading "You Are On Native Land," is a reminder of whose turf you are on. The menu is a kaleidoscope of colors, flavors, and textures not found in any old restaurant: highly seasonal dishes could include cricket seed mix with sunflower brittle, hand-harvested wild rice, or Labrador Tea Custard. There is always indigenous game, fish, birds, insects, wild plants, and heirloom varieties from Native American farms. There is never dairy, wheat flour, cane sugar, beef, chicken, or pork—colonial foods introduced and not originally from this land.

Naturally, the drinks program would have to follow a similar intentionality.

Originally, the restaurant was not planning to serve alcohol at all, due to stigma around alcohol and Native American communities. But due to their partnership contract with the Minneapolis Park and Recreation Board, they decided to serve beer and wine, along with an intricate menu of nonalcoholic drinks and teas.

All of Owamni's beer and wine is sourced first from BIPOC produc-ers, a difficult proposition in itself. "Alcohol has a very colonial, capi-talistic history," says Sherman. "Out of the 70-something breweries in Minnesota, we were only able to find one BIPOC producer, a Latinx producer called La Doña. It's super evident how little diversity there is because alcohol production is all about land access."

For wine, Owamni reached out to many people asking about Black or Indigenous producers and were ultimately able to find a small list of California wines, and some like Bruma, coming out of Mexico's Valle de Guadalupe. A few from South Africa, as well as some Māori wines out of New Zealand round out the list.

They also proudly offer zero-ABV cocktails, not with sugar water at their base, but instead wild teas using plants like hyssop, bergamot, Labrador, rose hips, and dried berries. "We really wanted the bever-age program to reflect and utilize wild flavors and have them taste like where we happen to be," explains Sherman. "We're trying to have more flavors like herbaceous and bitter mixed with sweet. Aronia berry, wild rice, corn. We're experimenting with the question of 'What are *modern* Indigenous beverages?'"

Delicious, that's what.

The recipes that follow are best made and shared in batches and are created by Owamni's *Anishinaabekweg* (Ojibway-Women) led bar team.

MANOOMIN (N/A)

OWAMNI

420 S 1ST ST., MINNEAPOLIS, MN 55401

Wild rice in Ojibwe, *manoomin* is extremely culturally significant to the tribe. Combined here with herbs and spices, this drink is as nutritious as it is tasty.

GLASSWARE: Large lowball glass

GARNISH: Puffed Wild Rice (see recipe)

- 3 tablespoons cinchona bark
- 3 tablespoons Mexican sarsaparilla
- 2 tablespoons maple sarsaparilla tea blend
- 1 ½ tablespoons spiceberry
- 1 tablespoon hawthorne berry
- 5 quarts hemp milk (for spices)
- 16 oz. hand-harvested wild rice
- 2 quarts hemp milk (for wild rice)

1. Grind all of the spices with a mortar and pestle.
2. Place the spices into the hemp milk, then bring the milk to a low simmer.
3. Simmer for 45 minutes, being careful not to let the milk boil.
4. As the spices are cooking, simmer the wild rice with 2 quarts hemp milk until the rice is cooked. Do not let the milk boil.
5. Once cooled, blend all of the ingredients together.
6. Strain the cocktail and squeeze thoroughly.
7. Serve chilled.

PUFFED WILD RICE: Put a handful of wild rice into a dry skillet over high heat. The rice will begin to "pop." Remove the rice from heat and let it cool.

BASHKODEJIBIK (N/A)

OWAMNI

420 S 1ST ST., MINNEAPOLIS, MN 55401

O jibwe for "sage," *bashkodejibik* is used for cleansing, ceremony, and blessing. Combined with nettles and bergamot, this is a curative drink made fun and fruity with berries.

GLASSWARE: Tapered collins glass
GARNISH: Candied Sage

- 4 tablespoons fresh sage
- 1 teaspoon dried white pine
- 1 tablespoon dried nettle
- 5 quarts water
- 2 ½ tablespoons wild ginger, peeled and cut into large chunks
- 1 tablespoon dried bergamot
- ½ pound blackberries
- 3 tablespoons frozen cranberries

1. Place sage, white pine, and nettle into a tea bag.
2. Combine all of the ingredients, except for the berries, in a pot.
3. Bring the mixture to a boil, then turn off the heat.
4. Remove the tea bag after 2 minutes.
5. Remove the ginger after 10 minutes.
6. Remove the mixture from heat and strain.
7. Cool the mixture.
8. Add the berries and blend them into the liquid with an immersion blender.
9. Strain the cocktail, allow it to cool, and serve into tapered collins glasses over ice.

PALMER'S BAR

500 CEDAR AVE., MINNEAPOLIS, MN 55454

Palmer's Bar is legend. It has sat since 1906 on Cedar Avenue on the West Bank of Minneapolis, in what must be some kind of mystical energy vortex. Everyone is drawn to Palmer's, eventually. It's the Minneapolis ur-dive, the One, with a wildly diverse clientele. From their own mouth: "Palmer's has been described as a church for down-and-outers and those who romanticize them, a rare place where high and low rub elbows—bums and poets, thieves and slumming celebrities."

In the 1960s, Palmer's was the epicenter of the West Bank music scene, where hippies and folksters like Spider John Koerner and Ray Glover made their bones, heavily influencing a young Bob Zimmerman when he lived nearby for a spell. It's still that rare bar today where you can walk in almost nightly and hear the vitality of real people playing real music.

SHOT AND A BEER BACK

PALMER'S BAR
500 CEDAR AVE., MINNEAPOLIS, MN 55454

For the authentic Palmer's experience, look no further. Throw these back immediately upon arrival, and let the neon signs become a bit glowier at the edges of your vision.

RECIPE: Equal parts Shut, Up, and Drink. Beer is so your other hand doesn't get lonely. Refill whenever necessary (preferably often).

THE PALMLOMA

PALMER'S BAR
500 CEDAR AVE., MINNEAPOLIS, MN 55454

The Palmer's take on the Paloma is downright delicious and typically unpretentious, with a splash of Fiesta Punch rounding out the grapefruit.

RECIPE: Equal parts reposado tequila, grapefruit juice, soda water and fiesta. Garnish with lime.

P.S. STEAK

510 GROVELAND AVE., MINNEAPOLIS, MN 55403

Located in one of the most storied restaurant spaces in Minneapolis—
the historic 510 Groveland building—P.S. Steak is old-school elegance
wrapped in a modern vibe. Stunning chandeliers, ornate woodwork,
velvet banquettes, and well-appointed serveware set a grand scene
for the classic steak house menu. But while the cocktail recipes skew
traditional, the PS Steak team uses contemporary techniques, ingredients, and influences that highlight local products and producers.

"Because we have four seasons, seasonality and nature can play a large part in inspiring bartenders," says Mike Liay, beverage director for Jester Concepts, which owns P.S. Steak. "Our major urban centers are not far from the great outdoors, so freshly grown or foraged ingredients can be the star. Beautiful fresh herbs like sweet gallium in the spring, delicious produce like fresh berries and apples in the summer and autumn, and a strong Nordic influence and ingredients during the winter months—all of that drive and creativity can be combined with local spirits from our burgeoning distilling scene for a wholly Minnesota cocktail."

FROZEN VODKA MARTINI

P.S. STEAK
510 GROVELAND AVE., MINNEAPOLIS, MN 55403

We build this Martini ahead of time, including dilution, for efficient and consistent service, says Mike Liay, beverage director. "Then we stash it in the freezer, pouring each one to order to ensure it arrives at the table perfectly chilled."

GLASSWARE: Cocktail glass, chilled
GARNISH: Olive, cocktail onion

- 50 ml vodka
- 15 ml Dolin Dry Vermouth
- 3 ml olive brine
- 3 drops Japanese Bitters Company Umami Bitters

1. Combine all of the ingredients over ice in a cocktail shaker or mixing glass.

2. Stir with ice.

3. Strain the cocktail into a chilled cocktail glass.

4. Garnish with an olive and cocktail onion on a skewer.

DUNBAR'S NUMBERS

P.S. STEAK
510 GROVELAND AVE., MINNEAPOLIS, MN 55403

This recipe can also be scaled up as a punch for parties—just omit the shaking and add sparkling sake right before guests arrive, says Liay.

GLASSWARE: Punch cup

- 120 ml hibiscus tea
- 45 ml bitter orange liqueur
- 30 ml vodka
- 30 ml sparkling sake
- 22 ml lychee liqueur
- 22 ml blanc vermouth
- 15 ml fresh citrus

1. Combine all of the ingredients, except for the sparkling sake, in a shaker.

2. Shake with ice.

3. Add the sparkling sake.

4. Strain the cocktail into a punch cup with a large ice cube.

RIVA TERRACE

245 HENNEPIN AVE., MINNEAPOLIS, MN 55401

When it's warm outside, the rooftop at Four Seasons Hotel Minneapolis resembles something out of *White Lotus*: an escape to the Italian Riviera, with a poppy, orange-and-cream color palette, vintage-inspired serveware and accessories, and sweeping views of Minneapolis. When the weather turns cold, the space morphs into Nordic Village, a collection of eight cabin-inspired huts outfitted for dining with a food and beverage menu that warms you from the inside—while the snow and wind stay outside. Minnesotans love to brave the winter elements, after all, but it's even better when you can stay warm.

CRYSTAL PALACE

RIVA TERRACE
245 HENNEPIN AVE., MINNEAPOLIS, MN 55401

The ideal cocktail for poolside afternoons spent taking in the expansive Minneapolis skyline.

GLASSWARE: Acrylic wine glass
GARNISH: Orange wheel half

- 75 ml Zardetto Prosecco
- 75 ml 3LECHE Ispahan FBB
- 20 ml Cappelletti Aperitivo
- 10 ml simple syrup

1. Combine all of the ingredients over pebble ice in a wine glass.

2. Garnish with a halved orange wheel.

ORANGE MOON

RIVA TERRACE
245 HENNEPIN AVE., MINNEAPOLIS, MN 55401

This cocktail is full of local flavors, as it's made with Brother Justus whiskey, as well as a collaboration coffee liqueur from Brother Justus and local roaster The Get Down Coffee Co.

GLASSWARE: Rocks glass
GARNISH: Perfect cara cara orange wedge

- 35 ml Allora Rosso Vermouth
- 35 ml Brother Justus American Single Malt Whiskey
- 15 ml Brother Justus x The Get Down Coffee Liqueur

1. Combine all of the ingredients in a small cocktail shaker.

2. Fill the shaker with ice and stir.

3. Strain the cocktail into a rocks glass.

4. Garnish with a Perfect cara cara orange wedge.

SIDEBAR AT SURDYK'S

303 E HENNEPIN AVE. #2, MINNEAPOLIS, MN 55414

The Surdyk name is synonymous with the Twin Cities food and beverage world. Started in 1934 by Joseph Surdyk—who bought one of the first legal liquor licenses available in Minneapolis—this wine, spirits, and liquor shop has been passed down through three generations, with each one making its mark. Joseph's son, Bill, moved the shop down the street to its current location and added more volume. His son, Jim, opened a cheese shop with global selections and also elevated the wine selection with more small production bottles, as well as wines from South Africa, Spain, and Chile. Along the way, the Surdyk family has been instrumental in helping to change Minnesota's archaic liquor laws.

Now, the current generation—Molly, Melissa, and Taylor—is growing the Surdyk's imprint. They launched an award-winning market and wine bar at Minneapolis-St. Paul airport, and in 2022 they opened Sidebar, a modern brasserie that's adjacent to the iconic store. Sidebar's wine, beer, and craft cocktail menu—as well as the modern bistro food menu—use the same products that are available on the shelves next door, allowing guests to discover new favorites and grab them on the way out—or just restock preferred spirits before heading home. It's a one-stop shop in the best possible way. Here's a Q&A with Molly Surdyk.

Why did your family decide to open Sidebar?

We had a lot of success at the airport, and we wanted to do something that people didn't need a plane ticket to get to, that was more accessible in general. We strive to have the best customer service and it's fun to sell products and talk about them with customers, but we never got to see people enjoy them. We also wanted a place where we could say to people, "We have that over at Sidebar, you can try it there." We looked at a lot of spaces and decided, what better place to open than the building we've occupied since the 1970s?

How does it complement the store?

We take what's in the cheese shop and the liquor store and put it all together at the restaurant. If you've found a wine you really liked here, you can just hop next door and get it. We want to make it very universal. I like to say, "Thanks for joining us, exit through our gift shop," because we carry so many things from the menu. We're very intentional in everything we put on our menu and everything we put on our shelves, and we want people to learn and love all of these things as much as we do.

How did you put together the cocktail list?

We had a lot of different influence and our cocktail list stemmed from our relationship with Alex at Sharab Shrubs, as well as my brother Taylor, who is our liquor buyer in the store. So we incorporate new and up-and-coming things while staying approachable but fun. We juice everything from scratch, and we put a lot of love in every single cocktail we do. There's a lot of intention in each one.

Your family has just been so influential in the Twin Cities. How do you continue that?

That was another reason we opened Sidebar: we want to keep growing in different ways. Things are always changing in the liquor and wine world, and the way people approach eating and drinking is always different. My dad opened the cheese shop, which was unheard of at the time. We branched into catering from there, then we were approached by MSP airport to open up a spot there. So we have always been growing and finding a different way to stay relevant while keeping true to our values.

MARTINI ESPRESS

SIDEBAR AT SURDYK'S
303 E HENNEPIN AVE. #2, MINNEAPOLIS, MN 55414

A house-made vanilla mocha syrup adds smooth, sweet flavors to this coffee-based drink.

GLASSWARE: Vintage coupe glass
GARNISH: 3 espresso beans

- 1 ½ oz. Sobieski Vodka
- 1 oz. B+W espresso
- ½ oz. Du Nord Cafe Frieda Coffee Liqueur
- ½ oz. Vanilla Mocha Syrup (see recipe)

1. Combine all of the ingredients in a cocktail tin.

2. Shake.

3. Pour the cocktail into a coupe glass.

4. Garnish with three espresso beans.

VANILLA MOCHA SYRUP: In a saucepan, combine 20 oz. water, 600 grams turbinado sugar, 42 grams coffee beans, 22 grams cocoa powder, and 10 grams vanilla extract and bring the mixture to a boil. Turn off the heat and let it steep for 5 minutes. Strain the syrup.

DREAMSICLE

SIDEBAR AT SURDYK'S
303 E HENNEPIN AVE. #2, MINNEAPOLIS, MN 55414

This drink represents both the nostalgia and progression of the Surdyk's brand," Taylor Surdyk says. "The initial sip takes you back to the first time you tasted the ice cream treat, and the combination of orange wine and Future Gin represent the vibrant and trendy people living in Northeast Minneapolis."

GLASSWARE: Vintage coupe glass
GARNISH: Candied orange

- 1 oz. Future Gin
- ½ oz. Tattersall Orange Crema
- ½ oz. egg white
- ½ oz. Krasno Orange Wine
- ½ oz. fresh-squeezed orange juice
- ½ oz. simple syrup

1. Pour all of the ingredients into a cocktail tin.

2. Shake.

3. Pour the cocktail into a coupe glass.

4. Garnish with a candied orange.

HOT RUSH

SIDEBAR AT SURDYK'S
303 E HENNEPIN AVE. #2, MINNEAPOLIS, MN 55414

A t Sidebar, we incorporate many ingredients stocked in our liquor store and cheese shop," says co-owner Taylor Surdyk. "Not only does it create a nice synergy, it also gives us the opportunity to show guests creative ways to use the products we sell. The Hot Rush uses Cry Baby Craig's Hot Honey, a local product that brings the heat— which is welcomed on a cold Minnesota day."

GLASSWARE: Riedel double old-fashioned glass
GARNISH: Sil-gochu

- 1 ½ oz. Buffalo Trace Bourbon
- ¾ oz. Meyer lemon juice
- ¾ oz. Cry Baby Craig's Hot Honey

1. Combine all of the ingredients.

2. Stir.

3. Garnish with sil-gochu.

TERZO

Meaning "three" in Italian, Terzo is the third restaurant from the Broder family, a longtime fixture on the Twin Cities dining scene. Situated across the intersection of 50th and Penn from its sister restaurants, Terzo opened in 2013 with a wine and beer license only, thanks to an old Southwest Minneapolis zoning law that banned serving spirits in neighborhoods. The Broder family—along with other South Minneapolis restaurateurs—was instrumental in lobbying to change the laws, and in 2017, Terzo finally scored a full liquor license—but had to work in a space created for far less volume. "We created a cocktail program in a bar that was designed to pour wine and beer almost exclusively," says bar manager Adam Schepker. "But I find creativity can flourish when you're given constraints."

Working within the cozy confines, Adam and his team create simple, straightforward cocktails that are rooted in the Italian tradition of apertivo, with amari, vermouth, and other bittersweet liqueurs taking center stage both on their own and as the foundation of the cocktail menu. "Many people don't know that there's a whole spectrum of amari, ranging from super light and citrusy to intense and really dark," says Sophia Pulice, director of service and hospitality for Broders' Restaurants. "We have been able to build a program that showcases all types of amari."

Pair that with an Italian wine list and a menu that highlights the truest form of Italian dining—antipasti, primi, secondi, contorni, dolci—and visitors to Terzo are whisked into an Italian oasis, complete with a treasured tradition that we can all get on board with. "A spritz at 4 o'clock on a Tuesday is something Italians get to enjoy because it's part of their culture," says Adam. "We try to cultivate that here."

NEBBIA ROSA

TERZO
2221 W 50TH ST., MINNEAPOLIS, MN 55419

This drink is an excellent punctuation mark on any meal. Rich and frothy—thanks to a reverse shake technique—it features Braulio, an alpine-style amaro that's been made near the Swiss border for over a century using a secret recipe of more than 20 mountain botanicals.

❖

GLASSWARE: Nick & Nora, chilled

- **2 ½ oz. Braulio**
- **¼ oz. Bordiga Aperitivo**
- **Pinch salt**
- **Expressed lemon peel**

1. Combine all of the ingredients into a shaker tin over ice.
2. Shake for 10 seconds.
3. Strain the liquid into the small tin of the shaker.
4. Dump ice from the large tin.
5. Dry-shake the cocktail for 10 seconds.
6. Double-strain the cocktail through a mesh strainer into a chilled Nick & Nora glass.

SARDINIAN SPRITZ

TERZO
2221 W 50TH ST., MINNEAPOLIS, MN 55419

Mirto, a liqueur made from myrtle berries from Sardinia, gives this drink a blue-fruit bitterness. (Bonus: it's a low-ABV cocktail!)

GLASSWARE: Teku glass

GARNISH: Orange slice

- 1 ½ oz. Bresca Dorada Mirto
- ½ oz. lemon juice
- 1 squirt cardamom bitters

- 3 oz. prosecco
- 1 oz. soda water

1. Add the mirto, lemon juice, and bitters to a teku glass.

2. Fill the glass with ice.

3. Add the prosecco.

4. Top with soda water.

5. Garnish with an orange slice and serve with a straw.

VESTALIA HOSPITALITY

VESTALIAHOSPITALITY.COM

Chef Ann Kim's hospitality group includes the pizza-centric spots that have garnered her awards and international recognition—Young Joni, Pizzeria Lola, and Hello Pizza—along with globally influenced Mexican restaurant Sooki & Mimi. But in-the-know Minneapolitans understand that the Ann Kim experience doesn't stop there. Young Joni and Sooki & Mimi both have adjacent cocktail lounges that are incognito on the outside, uniquely cozy on the inside, and serve precisely made craft cocktails that feature the same approach to global ingredients as the food menus.

ACAPULCO

BASEMENT BAR AT SOOKI & MIMI
1432 W 31ST ST., MINNEAPOLIS, MN 55408

Accessible in the alley behind Sooki & Mimi in Uptown and located beneath the restaurant, the Basement Bar is modeled after just that—your grandparents' basement. Low ceilings, comfortable couches and seats with retro patterns, a vintage turntable and reel-to-reel tape deck, and 1970s décor transport drinkers to an earlier era. Tacos provide sustenance, while the cocktail menu includes a dose of nostalgia. Just like grandma and grandpa's house, you won't want to leave.

This version of the classic tiki drink is big on flavor without leaning too heavily on sweetness. It's nostalgic and modern, all in one glass. For the rum, choose Appleton Estate, Hamilton, or Smith & Cross.

GLASSWARE: Coupe glass

GARNISH: Pineapple frond

- 2 oz. fresh pineapple juice
- 1 oz. reposado tequila
- 1 oz. Jamaican rum
- 1 oz. fresh grapefruit juice
- 1 dash green Tabasco sauce, plus more to taste

1. Fill a cocktail shaker with ice.

2. Add all of the ingredients.

3. Shake well until the shaker tin is cold and frosty.

4. Strain the cocktail into a coupe glass.

5. Serve garnished with a pineapple frond.

REEL-TO-REEL SLING

THE BACK BAR AT YOUNG JONI
165 13TH AVE. NE, MINNEAPOLIS, MN 55413

Young Joni's adjacent cocktail lounge is indicated by a small red light in the rear alley. Inside, the Northwoods cabin–inspired spot features floral wallpaper, vintage photos and artwork, retro dining room chairs, low tables, and couches. Unfinished wood walls and ceilings give a rustic vibe, and the cleverly themed menus—think high school yearbook and *TV Guide*—showcase precisely made cocktails that use unexpected flavors and ingredients. It's the perfect place to settle in with friends and continue the conversation over just one more drink.

Familiar enough for the casual drinker but with enough intrigue for the aficionado, this crushable cocktail is inspired by a Whiskey-Ginger with a punchy, bitter, and herbaceous twist. For the ginger syrup, use Liber & Co., and you can substitute Carpano Antica for the vermouth given here.

GLASSWARE: Collins glass
GARNISH: Lime wheel

- 2 oz. GT's Hibiscus Ginger Kombucha
- 1 ½ oz. bourbon
- ¾ oz. lime juice
- ½ oz. ginger syrup
- ½ oz. Punt e Mes
- 2 dashes Bittermens Hellfire Shrub Bitters

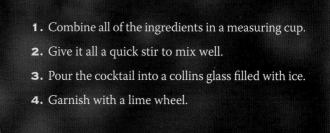

1. Combine all of the ingredients in a measuring cup.

2. Give it all a quick stir to mix well.

3. Pour the cocktail into a collins glass filled with ice.

4. Garnish with a lime wheel.

VOLSTEAD'S EMPORIUM

711 W LAKE ST., MINNEAPOLIS, MN 55408

Tucked in an alley around the corner from the Lyn-Lake intersection, Volstead's is a classic vintage speakeasy—right down to the blink-and-you'll-miss-it red lightbulb that indicates its existence. Inside, the subterranean spot takes guests back to an earlier time, with dark woodwork, dim lighting, vintage details, and speakeasy-style features like two-way mirrors and hidden rooms.

Bar manager Marley Bartlett and her team craft cocktails that not only meet the unique surroundings, but elevate it, drawing on cocktail inspiration from an earlier time—but giving the menu a decidedly modern feel.

What makes the Volstead's cocktail menu unique?

Our menu is based on classic cocktails from the 1920s. Our staff gets to research and develop together and come up with riffs on the classics that feature new and exciting ingredients. I love that our menu is made by our staff and not just one person.

How does the cocktail menu fit the space?

We keep it classic to the 1920s Prohibition era. We are a speakeasy, and our menu has drinks you would imagine from that time period, from a booze-forward Old Fashioned to a mesmerizing Green Fairy Absinthe. It's very fitting for our red-velvet, moody basement.

What makes the Twin Cities cocktail scene special?

Honestly, the liquor reps we have in the Twin cities make the cocktail scene so special. I have high praise for my reps that are always willing to bring in interesting spirits to broaden our menu and expand our knowledge. I also love all our local distilleries that produce amazing products, and to put them on our menu is an amazing way to support them.

BITTER BUTTERFLY

VOLSTEAD'S EMPORIUM
711 W LAKE ST., MINNEAPOLIS, MN 55408

This cocktail is Volstead's riff on the classic Paper Plane.

GLASSWARE: Coupe glass

- 25 ml Four Roses Bourbon
- 25 ml Aperol
- 25 ml Averna Amaro
- 20 ml lemon juice
- 15 ml ginger simple syrup

1. Pour all of the ingredients into a cocktail shaker.

2. Shake together.

3. Serve up in a coupe glass.

168 — TWIN CITIES COCKTAILS

VOLSTEAD'S OLD FASHIONED

VOLSTEAD'S EMPORIUM
711 W LAKE ST., MINNEAPOLIS, MN 55408

It's the first drink that Marley Bartlett made for the menu, and it's a perennial favorite.

GLASSWARE: Old-fashioned glass

GARNISH: Flamed orange peel

- 60 ml Four Roses Bourbon
- 3 dashes Angonar (a blend of Angostura bitters and Cynar)
- 5 ml Smoked Demerara Syrup (see recipe)

1. Add all of the ingredients together in a cocktail shaker.

2. Shake to combine.

3. Pour the cocktail over rocks into an old-fashioned glass.

4. Garnish with a flamed orange peel.

SMOKED DEMERARA SYRUP: Make one overflowing barspoon (about 5 ml) of 1:1 demerara syrup, then smoke it with a smoking gun with applewood chips.

ST. PAUL

BRUNSON'S PUB

CAN CAN WONDERLAND

EMERALD LOUNGE

THE LEXINGTON

PAJARITO

As a born-and-raised St. Paulite, I'm more than accustomed to jokes—some of them true—about my native city being the smaller, more provincial sister to big city Minneapolis. That said, any trip to the Twin Cities is not complete without a visit to both cities. They may not be twins in any actuality, but they are sisters, and little sis should never be underestimated.

By most accounts, St. Paul is extremely "liveable"— affordable, amiable, diverse, charming, and in many sections not victim to over-gentrification. What this means for the bar scene is a friendly, affable vibe. Think long-standing neighborhood corner dives, Irish pubs, burger-and-beer joints, red sauce grandes dames, and places where pool tables, pull tabs, and bingo cards reign supreme.

But please do not take this to mean that all of the dad jokes about "keeping St. Paul boring" are true. "Small Paul" is also home to some of the prettiest and most elegant hotel bars around—see our eponymous St. Paul Hotel, or Celeste of St. Paul, housed in a former convent.

Like any good city, St. Paul can't be defined by any single broad stroke—only that it should not be overlooked in favor of its more famous sibling.

—Mecca Bos

BRUNSON'S PUB

956 PAYNE AVE., ST. PAUL, MN 55130

Brunson's has been a bar of some stripe or another since Prohibition. It's situated in a stretch of St. Paul traditionally known for being blue-collar, which has now transformed into one of the most rapidly diversifying, least pretentious, and genuinely cool neighborhoods in either city. And Brunson's is a pure reflection of that.

Owners Thomas and Molly LaFleche were lifer bartenders with one dream and one dream only: To have a bar of their own.

Brunson's is that bar, made by and for people who believe in the life-affirming power of a quality libation and a friendly face to pour it, at a decent price. It's that simple.

The kitchen is run by a Black chef, Torrance Beavers, who helms a nearly all-Black kitchen—a rarity in a Twin Cities restaurant. The diversity is intentional; everyone in question wants the inside of Brunson's to look like a true reflection of the community outside.

That inside features an original mahogany bar, 13-foot ceilings, and hardwood floors that have seen it all, making Brunson's feel like the bar you want to drink at, will always drink at, and fits all occasions, from wholesome family gatherings to a quick one after work and everything in between.

Another reason to visit Brunson's? Its Payne Avenue location, an all-too-rare stretch of American road where most businesses are still indie and authentic. What you will find on a stroll down Payne is a combination coffee shop/record store, a Mexican butcher shop, a Black-owned barber shop, and a 100-year-old cash-only liquor store/Italian market, among many other gems.

Go for the strolling, stay to sip a cocktail or two at Brunson's.

BENNY'S OLD FASHIONED

BRUNSON'S PUB
956 PAYNE AVE., ST. PAUL, MN 55130

Any proper bar needs a house Old Fashioned, and this is Brunson's. With peppercorn simle syrup there's nothing fusty about it.

GLASSWARE: Old-fashioned glass

GARNISH: Expressed orange peel

- **2 oz. rye whiskey**
- **1 oz. Tattersall Sour Cherry Liqueur**
- **1 teaspoon peppercorn simple syrup**
- **2 dashes Angostura bitters**

1. Combine the ingredients in an old-fashioned glass and stir over ice.

2. Squeeze orange peel over glass to express.

3. Garnish with an expressed orange peel.

CORPSE REVIVER #2

BRUNSON'S PUB
956 PAYNE AVE., ST. PAUL, MN 55130

Whether it's a hangover "cure" or not is debatable, but if you're going to have hair of the dog, it might as well taste as dreamy as this orange-inflected reviver.

GLASSWARE: Coupe glass, chilled
GARNISH: Expressed lemon peel

- Absinthe, to rinse
- ¾ oz. Tattersall Gin
- ¾ oz. Tattersall Orange Crema
- ¾ oz. Cocchi Americano
- ¾ oz. fresh lemon juice
- ¾ oz. simple syrup

1. Rinse the inside of a chilled coupe glass with absinthe.

2. Add the remaining ingredients to a shaker with ice.

3. Shake until well chilled.

4. Strain the cocktail into the coupe glass.

5. Garnish with an expressed lemon peel.

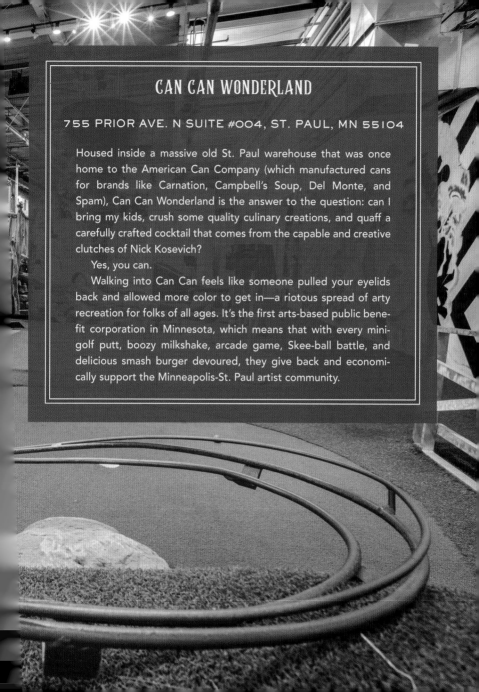

CAN CAN WONDERLAND

755 PRIOR AVE. N SUITE #004, ST. PAUL, MN 55104

Housed inside a massive old St. Paul warehouse that was once home to the American Can Company (which manufactured cans for brands like Carnation, Campbell's Soup, Del Monte, and Spam), Can Can Wonderland is the answer to the question: can I bring my kids, crush some quality culinary creations, and quaff a carefully crafted cocktail that comes from the capable and creative clutches of Nick Kosevich?

Yes, you can.

Walking into Can Can feels like someone pulled your eyelids back and allowed more color to get in—a riotous spread of arty recreation for folks of all ages. It's the first arts-based public bene-fit corporation in Minnesota, which means that with every mini-golf putt, boozy milkshake, arcade game, Skee-ball battle, and delicious smash burger devoured, they give back and economi-cally support the Minneapolis-St. Paul artist community.

BUBBLE UP

CAN CAN WONDERLAND
755 PRIOR AVE. N SUITE #004, ST. PAUL, MN 55104

Don't let the aroma of the garnish fool you, with its ability to time-warp you back to lazy childhood summers of baseball and Big League Chew—there's a deliciously boozy drink in here, all wrapped up in a stupidly fun package.

GLASSWARE: Soda fountain
GARNISH: Bubble Gum Air (see recipe)

- 4 oz. seltzer
- 2 oz. Garden Variety Sour Mix
- 1 ½ oz. Earl Giles Vodka
- ½ oz. banana rum

1. Combine all of the ingredients in a shaker.

2. Pour the cocktail over crushed ice.

3. Garnish with Bubble Gum Air.

BUBBLE GUM AIR
Combine 1 teaspoon Foam Magic, 200 ml water, 60 ml sour mix, and 2 ml seltzer and blend with a stick blender until foam appears. Collect the foam.

EMERALD LOUNGE

455 7TH ST. W, ST. PAUL, MN 55102

West 7ᵗʰ Street is a long, slashing historic thoroughfare that cuts a six-mile diagonal along the Mississippi, beginning in downtown St. Paul and ending near the airport. Along the way, remnants of the city's beer-soaked, blue-collar past loom. The old Schmidt Brewery, in all its gothic red brick glory, is now converted into artist lofts. Dive bars old and new appear between the car washes and fast-food joints, and newer brewhouses like the German-focused Waldmann Brewery nod to tradition.

Recently, a newer energy has taken hold of the West 7ᵗʰ neighborhood. Drawn by more affordable real estate and cheaper rents, younger business owners are shaking things up, and the Emerald Lounge is a perfect example of that: an intimate, vibrant cocktail bar and lounge, blazing with life right in the midst of so much entropy, staking a claim for the growing vitality of the neighborhood.

Thankfully, the Emerald happens to be mixing some of the best cocktails in town. You'll often find notable local bartenders bellying up post-shift, which is how you know it's good.

THE HUNTRESS

EMERALD LOUNGE
455 7TH ST. W, ST. PAUL, MN 55102

This savory take on a Gibson was named after bar manager Vincent's cat, Blanca, "because she was good at killing things."

GLASSWARE: Nick & Nora glass, chilled
GARNISH: Pickled red onion, boquerones

- 1 ½ oz. dill-infused aquavit
- 1 oz. London dry gin
- ½ oz. dry vermouth
- 6 dashes white balsamic vinegar
- 6 drops saline solution

1. Stir all of the ingredients together thoroughly in a well-chilled mixing glass.

2. Strain the cocktail into a chilled Nick & Nora.

3. Garnish with a pickled onion and boquerones.

ANNE WITH AN E

EMERALD LOUNGE
455 7TH ST. W, ST. PAUL, MN 55102

Tart, dry, and austere with a silky-smooth texture and an herbaceous nose, this drink is named after Vincent's late mother, Anne.

GLASSWARE: Coupe glass, chilled
GARNISH: Edible flower petal

- 2 oz. London dry gin
- ¾ oz. lemon juice
- ¾ oz. egg white
- ½ oz. dry curaçao

- ½ oz. honey syrup
- 2 drops saline solution
- Grapefruit peel
- Green Chartreuse, to atomize

1. Add all of the ingredients, except for the Green Chartreuse, and a large piece of grapefruit peel to your shaking tin.

2. Dry-shake vigorously for 10 to 15 seconds.

3. Add ice and shake vigorously for 10 to 15 seconds.

4. Double-strain the cocktail into a chilled coupe glass.

5. Atomize with Green Chartreuse.

6. Garnish with an edible flower petal.

THE LEXINGTON

1096 GRAND AVE., ST. PAUL, MN 55105

A historic restaurant in a historic St. Paul neighborhood, the 75-year-old institution—a former speakeasy—radiates old-school elegance. The restaurant's rooms set a stunning scene for everything from business lunches to family occasions, while classic cocktails accompany a traditional steak house menu—both heavy on local ingredients—and are delivered with detail-oriented service that also evokes an earlier time.

THE WILLIAMSBURG

THE LEXINGTON
1096 GRAND AVE., ST. PAUL, MN 55105

This variation on a classic Manhattan is made with amaro and chocolate bitters for added depth.

GLASSWARE: Coupe glass
GARNISH: Luxardo cherry on a pick

- 3 oz. George Dickel American Rye Whiskey
- ½ oz. Carpano Antica Formula Vermouth
- ½ oz. Amaro Montenegro
- 6 dashes cocoa bitters

1. Combine all of the ingredients in a cocktail tin.

2. Stir.

3. Pour the cocktail into a coupe glass.

4. Garnish with a pick through a Luxardo cherry.

GRAPEFRUIT NEGRONI

THE LEXINGTON
1096 GRAND AVE., ST. PAUL, MN 55105

T he Lexington's version of a classic Negroni features locally made grapefruit liqueur from Tattersall Distillery for a unique twist.

GLASSWARE: Double old-fashioned glass

GARNISH: Orange peel

- 1 oz. London dry gin
- 1 oz. Tattersall Grapefruit Crema
- ½ oz. Carpano Antica Formula Vermouth
- ½ oz. Campari

1. Combine all of the ingredients in a cocktail tin.

2. Stir them together.

3. Pour the cocktail into a double old-fashioned glass over one large ice cube.

4. Garnish with an orange peel.

PAJARITO

605 7TH ST. W, ST. PAUL, MN 55102

This upscale Mexican bistro has two locations—in St. Paul on historic West 7th, and in Edina at the posh 50th and France area—bringing Mexico's treasured regional cuisines and cooking traditions to both neighborhoods, complete with twists on the Margarita and other traditional Mexican cocktails. The bar program also features an extensive list of curated agave spirits, from well-known options to rare liquors that guests won't find anywhere else.

LAST CORPSE

PAJARITO
605 7TH ST. W, ST. PAUL, MN 55102

T he Last Corpse is an homage to two classics: the Corpse Reviver and the Last Word. The brightness of the vermouth compliments the herbaceous elements of the Green Chartreuse, and because Alex Quamme, bar manager at the Edina location, uses mezcal instead of gin, there are smoky undertones. The result is a well-balanced, citrusy cocktail that's not too sweet with lots of depth.

GLASSWARE: Coupe glass
GARNISH: Lime twist

- Absinthe, to spritz
- 1 ¼ oz. La Luna Cupreata
- 1 oz. lime juice

- ¾ oz. Cocchi Americano
- ¾ oz. Green Chartreuse
- ½ oz. rosemary syrup

1. Spritz the inside of a couple glass once or twice with absinthe. (An absinthe rinse will also work.)

2. In a shaker tin, add all of the remaining ingredients.

3. Add ice and shake.

4. Double-strain the cocktail into the coupe glass using a classic cocktail strainer and a small fine-mesh strainer.

5. Garnish with a lime twist.

HABANERO CILANTRO MARGARITA

PAJARITO
605 7TH ST. W, ST. PAUL, MN 55102

T his spicy, refreshing Margarita is a welcome break from overly sweet or fruity versions, and is a staple on the cocktail menu.

GLASSWARE: Rocks glass
GARNISH: Thinly sliced habanero pepper, cilantro sprig

- Salt, for the rim
- Habanero Tincture (see recipe)
- 2 oz. El Jimador Reposado Tequila
- 1 oz. cilantro syrup
- ¾ oz. lime juice
- ½ oz. orange curaçao

1. Salt the rim of a rocks glass.

2. Add 2 to 4 dashes of habanero tincture, depending on your spice preference.

3. Combine all of the remaining ingredients in a shaker.

4. Add ice and shake.

5. Strain the cocktail into the glass and add ice.

6. Garnish with a slice of habanero and sprig of cilantro.

HABANERO TINCTURE: Slice two habaneros and place them in a glass jar. Add 2 oz. neutral grain spirit (a higher ABV will speed up the process). Seal the jar and store it in a cool, dark place for 3 days to 1 week. Filter the tincture into a new glass bottle using a coffee filter and funnel.

THE SUBURBS

BALDAMAR

GIANNI'S STEAKHOUSE

GETAWAY MOTOR CAFE

THE MUDD ROOM

MR. PAUL'S SUPPER CLUB

One of the best things about the Twin Cities Metro Area is that the suburbs have some truly excellent reasons to make the drive. While I'm partial to the 'burb where I grew up—Apple Valley—each one boasts a unique feel, with its own special culture, nature, innovation, and the occasional quirk or oddity.

But there's a few things that the suburbs all have in common: a lake or two (or a few), plenty of trails and green spaces (perfect for any season), and a vibrant and fun dining scene that doesn't have to be an also-ran to the cities.

Here is just a very small selection of what our suburbs have to offer. Whatever your preferred mode of transport—car, bus, light rail, or bike (there are trails heading in every direction)—head north, south, east, or west for a delicious adventure and discover what our surrounding areas are serving up.

—Molly Each

BALDAMAR

1642 COUNTY RD. B2 W, ROSEVILLE, MN 55113

Bold, flavorful, and focused on the details, the cocktail menu at Baldamar—a modern steak house in Roseville, just outside Minneapolis—features distinctive drinks that hold their own next to the restaurant's filet mignon, ribeye steak, miso-marinated seabass, and braised pork shank.

Led by beverage director Sean Merrill, along with senior lead bartenders Kenneth Kieck and Mary Jackson, both the cocktails and N/A offerings are inspired by the team's travels, as they discover new, high-end spirits—many that aren't available elsewhere in the state—to incorporate into cocktails that introduce something new to both novices and even the occasional aficionado.

Craft is the name of the game at Baldamar. To wit: The 14 Karrot Queen, an intensive, multi-step drink that's a staple of Sunday's Champagner Brunch, and the Neuske's Old Fashioned, which features Woodinville Bourbon washed in bacon fat over twenty-four hours. You know what they say: good things take time—especially when they're washed in bacon.

N.Y.F.O.F. (NOT YOUR FATHER'S OLD FASHIONED)

BALDAMAR
1642 COUNTY RD. B2 W, ROSEVILLE, MN 55113

The Baldamar bar team notes that you could smoke this cocktail for added drama and flavor. The piloncillo simple syrup is a Mexican fortified simple syrup.

GLASSWARE: Rocks glass
GARNISH: Expressed orange slice, cherry

- 2 oz. Baldamar Select Buffalo Trace Bourbon
- ¾ oz. piloncillo simple syrup
- 2 dashes cherry bark/vanilla bitters
- 1 dash orange bitters
- 1 drop vanilla extract

1. Stir together all of the ingredients.
2. Strain the cocktail into a rocks glass over a large ice cube.
3. Express a slice of orange into the cocktail.
4. Garnish with a cherry.

14 KARROT QUEEN

BALDAMAR
1642 COUNTY RD. B2 W, ROSEVILLE, MN 55113

This drink is a staple on Baldamar's luxe, all-you-can-eat—and all-you-can imbibe—Champagner Brunch. It requires a little extra effort, but rest assured: it pays off in both flavor and visual appeal.

GLASSWARE: Coupe glass
GARNISH: Dot of bitters, fresh sage leaf

- 1 oz. Hendrick's Gin
- ¾ oz. Tamarelo Tamarind Liqueur
- ½ oz. Barrow's Ginger Liqueur
- ½ oz. simple syrup
- ¾ oz. fresh carrot juice
- ¼ oz. fresh pineapple juice
- 3 dashes orange bitters
- 1 egg white

1. Over ice, shake the gin, tamarind liqueur, ginger liqueur, and simple syrup.
2. Strain the mixture into a second shaker.
3. Add the carrot and pineapple juices, bitters, and egg white.
4. Dry-shake to thoroughly froth the egg white.
5. Serve up the cocktail in a coupe glass.
6. Dot the top of the cocktail with bitters and drag though the bitters with a cocktail straw to create hearts.
7. As a final touch, express a fresh sage leaf and arrange opposite the bitters hearts.

PINEAPPLE PASSION DAIQUIRI

GIANNI'S STEAKHOUSE
635 LAKE ST. E, WAYZATA, MN 55391

S ince 1997, Gianni's has been serving old-school elegance and cocktails in Wayzata. Drinks like a Dirty Martini (see page 214) sit alongside new creations like this tropical drink. It's all part of the scene, with white tablecloths, chandeliers, a menu of farm-raised meats, and a team of seasoned servers.

GLASSWARE: Coupe glass

GARNISH: Disco lime

- 1 ¾ oz. pineapple rum
- 1 oz. passion fruit liqueur
- ¾ oz. simple syrup
- ½ oz. lime juice

1. Combine all of the ingredients over ice in a cocktail shaker.

2. Double-strain the cocktail into a coupe.

3. Garnish with a disco lime.

DIRTY MARTINI

GIANNI'S STEAKHOUSE
635 LAKE ST. E, WAYZATA, MN 55391

*C*risp, clean, slightly briny, and oh-so-simple. There's a reason this cocktail remains at the top of many a drinker's favorites list.

GLASSWARE: Martini glass, chilled
GARNISH: Olive on a skewer

- 3 oz. vodka or gin
- ½ oz. olive juice (or more depending on preference)

1. Pour the ingredients into a cocktail tin.

2. Shake.

3. Pour the cocktail into a chilled martini glass.

4. Garnish with an olive on a skewer.

MATCHA GIMLET

GETAWAY MOTOR CAFE
120 BROADWAY ST., CARVER, MN 55315

Located in historic Carver, Minnesota, Getaway Motor Cafe provides precisely made versions of both coffee and cocktails with a side of community involvement. The comfortable décor and friendly faces make it the kind of place you'll want to post up for coffee and pastries, then transition into cocktails and stay a while longer. Plus, it's even easier when the cocktail menu was created by local legend Nick Kosevich (see page 314). In this drink, the aggressively earthy notes of matcha are beautifully balanced here with a strong hit of lime.

GLASSWARE: Coupe glass
GARNISH: Candy tuile

- 2 oz. Earl Giles Vodka
- 1 ½ oz. Earl Giles Lime Elixir
- ½ oz. water
- 2 barspoons matcha latte powder
- 3 dashes Bittercube Orange Bitters

1. Combine all of the ingredients in a cocktail tin with ice.

2. Give the ingredients a long shake.

3. Double-strain the cocktail into a coupe glass.

4. Garnish with candy tuile.

THE MUDD ROOM

1352 STATE HWY 13, MENDOTA, MN 55150

Tucked beneath Lucky's 13 Pub in Mendota, Minnesota, The Mudd Room features the telltale signs of a dreamy, speakeasy-style spot: dark wood, etched glass, a 1920s mahogany bar, an intimate atmosphere, and vintage-inspired cocktails that have been given a dose of contemporary cocktail culture, and pair well with a menu of small plates that allow guests to order just one more. As for the name? It's a nod to the book *Saint Mudd*, by Steve Thayer, a novel about saints and gangers in the 1930s.

MACHINE GUN KELLY MANHATTAN

THE MUDD ROOM
1352 STATE HIGHWAY 13, MENDOTA, MN 55150

The contrast in temperatures between the chilled cocktail and the room-temperature amaro will help in floating the liqueur. To float the liqueur, pour it onto the spoon to disperse it gently across the top of the cocktail.

GLASSWARE: Martini glass
GARNISH: Filthy Black Cherry

- 1½ oz. Woodinville Straight Rye Whiskey
- ¼ oz. Drapò Sweet Vermouth, chilled
- ¼ oz. Tattersall Italiano
- 1 scoop Filthy Cherry Juice
- ¼ oz. Foro Amaro, room temperature, for the float

1. Combine all of the ingredients, except for the amaro, in a tin shaker with ice.

2. Stir, do not shake, the mixture, as shaking will bruise the booze.

3. Strain the cocktail into a martini glass over a big ice rock.

4. Using a spoon, float the amaro across the top of the cocktail.

5. Garnish with a Filthy Black Cherry (an Amarena cherry).

SOUL OF THE CITY

THE MUDD ROOM
1352 STATE HIGHWAY 13, MENDOTA, MN 55150

In this next-level vodka-cranberry concoction, tart cranberry juice gets an extra boost from locally made cranberry liqueur.

GLASSWARE: Collins glass
GARNISH: Lime wheel

- **2 oz. cranberry juice**
- **1 ½ oz. Tito's Vodka**
- **1 oz. Tattersall Cranberry Liqueur**
- **½ oz. fresh-squeezed lime juice**
- **½ oz. egg white**

1. Combine all of the ingredients in a metal cocktail shaker without ice.
2. Dry-shake until a froth is achieved.
3. Pour the cocktail over crushed ice into a collins glass.
4. Garnish with a fresh lime wheel.

MR. PAUL'S SUPPER CLUB SAZERAC

MR. PAUL'S SUPPER CLUB
3917 MARKET ST., EDINA, MN 55424

A dose of New Orleans in the heart of Edina, Mr. Paul's Supper Club takes the vibrant, delicious cuisine and culture from NOLA and wraps it in a traditional supper club setting, creating a spot that's ideal for date nights, big group dinners, and every outing in between. Standard New Orleans cocktails feature heavily, with modern ingredients and techniques amping up offerings like this Sazerac, which is livened up with house-made elements and elevated with some fun liquid nitogen technique.

GLASSWARE: Small rocks glass
GARNISH: Liquid nitrogen, Mr. Paul's Miracle Sazerac
Cocktail Enhancer

- 1 ½ oz. water
- 1 oz. rye whiskey
- 1 oz. cognac

- ¼ oz. fennel bittered piloncillo syrup
- 3 dashes Bittercube Orange Bitters
- 1 dash Peychaud's bitters

1. Combine all of the ingredients together in a mixing glass.

2. Pour 1 oz. liquid nitrogen into the bottom of a small rocks glass and spray 3 sprays of cocktail enhancer into the glass.

3. Add the cocktail ingredients to the glass.

4. Give it one more spray and serve.

HURRICANE

MR. PAUL'S SUPPER CLUB
3917 MARKET ST., EDINA, MN 55424

A slightly less sweet version of the New Orleans classic.

GLASSWARE: Hurricane glass
GARNISH: Bing cherry, umbrella

- 2 oz. Earl Giles Tropical Elixir
- 2 oz. water
- 1 oz. light rum

- 1 oz. dark rum
- ½ oz. Chinola Passion Fruit Liqueur

1. Combine all of the ingredients in a mixing glass.

2. Pour the cocktail into a hurricane glass over pebble ice.

3. Garnish with a Bing cherry and a cocktail umbrella.

DISTILLERIES

BROTHER JUSTUS WHISKEY COMPANY

DU NORD SOCIAL SPIRITS

EARL GILES DISTILLERY

O'SHAUGHNESSY DISTILLING CO.

RED LOCKS IRISH WHISKEY

TATTERSALL DISTILLING

TWIN SPIRITS DISTILLERY

The Twin Cities' Midwestern geography means we're surrounded by an abundance of fruits, vegetables, herbs, nuts, spices, and other plants that are indigenous to our area. Our chefs embraced the bounty, and the local and sustainable movement took off. Mixologists also turned to fresh flora as well, taking the farm-to-table philosophy to the glass.

Here, our locavore movement goes even deeper: Our many talented distillers are using these plants to craft unique spirits and N/A concoctions that give drinkers a taste of our history, culture, and cuisine in every single glass. Mix up one of these cocktails—courtesy of the distillers themselves—and raise a glass to supporting local down to the root.

BROTHER JUSTUS WHISKEY COMPANY

3300 5TH ST. NE, MINNEAPOLIS, MN 55418

This northeast Minneapolis distillery started crafting spirits in a small space in 2018, then opened their cocktail room in 2021, making it a relative newcomer to the scene. Founder/CEO Phil Steger and his team use time-honored techniques and locally sourced and foraged ingredients—all from within 125 miles of the distillery—to create whiskey that's 100-percent Minnesota made. It's served in a cozy cocktail room that's minimal yet rustic, and accented by plants, books, and floor-to-ceiling windows. It has the feel of a home featured on the pages of a design magazine—only with really good cocktails and bottles of whiskey to go.

Why did you start Brother Justus?

I created Brother Justus to distill Minnesota's vast and varied landscapes into a single, expansive sip. We handcraft all our whiskeys from whole ingredients—water, malted barley, white oak, and peat—sourced within 125 miles of our Minneapolis distillery.

What makes Brother Justus spirits unique?

That fact that our whiskeys are made from scratch using all Minnesota-sourced whole ingredients, following all-original recipes, with nothing sourced or blended. This is harder, but we want to make Minnesota the Single-Malt State the way Kentucky is the state of Bourbon. Plus, our Cold-Peated is the only whiskey in existence made with whole, millennia-old cold peat instead of burned peat smoke.

What makes the Twin Cities cocktail scene special?

Minnesota knows flavors. Our nationally recognized restaurants and chefs prove that. Our bars and cocktails are the same. We're a big city filled with creative, culturally diverse, and hard-working people who plant their traditions, cultures, and genius in Minnesota's deep soils and season them in our weather of spectacular extremes, producing whole new worlds of flavor. Minneapolis entrepreneur Houston White calls it "cultural collision."

What makes the Twin Cities distillery scene unique?

Minnesota's spirits history dates back to Prohibition, when Minnesotans were creating some of the best, most highly sought moonshine in the nation. A century's worth of small distillery-suppressing liquor laws means we distillers now have to hustle a little harder to make our businesses work. The result is a laboratory of diverse approaches producing a wide variety of exceptional spirits. Whatever you like best, someone in Minnesota is making one of the best versions of it.

Where do you like to have a drink in your off hours?

With the business and young kids, I spend a lot of time at the distillery and at home having cocktails with friends and family, or a quiet sip in a moment to myself. Still, there are tons of places I love. In Minneapolis: Young Joni, Northeast Social, Mara at the Four Seasons, and the Hewing Hotel. Plus, whatever project Nick Kosevich has going on. In St. Paul: Ngon Bistro, Dark Horse, W.A. Frost, and my personal dive bar heaven, The Spot.

COLD-PEATED OLD FASHIONED

BROTHER JUSTUS WHISKEY COMPANY
3300 5TH ST. NE, MINNEAPOLIS, MN 55418

The distillery's cold-peated whiskey shines in this classic cocktail. Using the only cold-peated method in the world—dubbed the Aitkin County Process—means that the herbaceous flavors of Minnesota-grown peat complement the smokey notes, instead of being overpowered.

GLASSWARE: Rocks glass

GARNISH: Orange peel

- 2 oz. Brother Justus Cold-Peated Whiskey
- ½ oz. simple syrup
- 2 dashes Angostura bitters

1. Combine the whiskey, simple syrup, and bitters in a mixing glass.
2. Stir with a barspoon until the syrup has dissolved into the whiskey.
3. Add one large cube or a few small cubes to the rocks glass.
4. Pour the drink into the rocks glass.
5. Express the orange peel over the cocktail to release its oils.
6. Add the garnish and serve.

AFTERNOONS WITH ANNIE

BROTHER JUSTUS WHISKEY COMPANY
3300 5TH ST. NE, MINNEAPOLIS, MN 55418

Brother Justus's American Single Malt Whiskey features notes of toasted oak, butterscotch, and stone fruit. In this cocktail, they seamlessly blend with coffee, blackberry, mint, and lemon, creating a drink that expertly balances rich and bright flavors.

GLASSWARE: Rocks glass
GARNISH: Mint sprig, blackberries

- 1 ½ oz. Brother Justus American Whiskey
- 1 oz. Afternoons with Annie Syrup (see recipe)
- 1 oz. cold brew coffee
- ½ oz. lemon juice

1. Combine all of the ingredients in a cocktail tin.

2. Shake vigorously for 10 seconds.

3. Strain the cocktail into a rocks glass with ice.

4. Garnish with a mint sprig and blackberries.

AFTERNOONS WITH ANNIE SYRUP: Combine 1 cup water, 1 cup sugar, 100 grams blackberries, and 12 grams dried spearmint in a pot and bring the mixture to a boil, stirring until incorporated. Once boiling, reduce the heat to a low simmer and let simmer for 20 minutes. Filter the mixture through a fine-mesh strainer. Add the liquid to a blender with 100 grams blackberries and blend on high for 15 seconds to puree. Filter the syrup through a fine-mesh strainer. Chill. Store the syrup and use for up to 2 weeks.

DU NORD SOCIAL SPIRITS

2610 E 32ND ST., MINNEAPOLIS, MN 55406

As the first (legal) Black-owned distillery in the United States, and the only one in Minnesota, Du Nord Social Spirits is already unique. But that's just part of their story.

During the events surrounding George Floyd's murder, Du Nord's plant and cocktail room were partially destroyed in the uprising. It was then that founder Chris Montana decided he would start a foundation to help the community.

"We want to create positive change for people who might not otherwise get to experience a lot of positivity," Montana says.

But don't think that just because Du Nord does good that it doesn't also *taste* good. Minnesotans, including our hometown hub airline Delta—where the spirits are highlighted—ask for the label by name.

The distillery's beginnings are humble. Montana was graduating from law school and found out that he was going to be a father for the first time.

"I won't say we were *completely* broke, because I've been completely broke, and I know what that's like. But we weren't exactly stacking paper."

Montana's wife Shanelle's family had a farm, and Chris got an idea: Grain from that farm could be distilled, and the result could make them some much-needed paper. So, they started making a vodka, now called Foundation, and sales support the foundation.

But, he says, that first year was hands-down the most difficult of his life: twenty-two-hour workdays and fifteen-minute power naps for the remaining two in the distillery. He doesn't like the glamorization of that kind of grind culture, even though he—and the company—got through it.

"It shouldn't be that hard."

That's where the Du Nord Foundation comes in, by addressing racial inequities and building economic justice in the Twin Cities and offering immediate financial relief, as well as long-term investments, in entrepreneurs and business leaders of color. "We've always been focused on craft spirits and quality in the bottle, but we've never been about just making money. We want to show up in ways that matter for other people."

Though their beloved, community-oriented cocktail room closed during the confluence of the pandemic and George Floyd's murder, Du Nord has big plans for 2023 and 2024. By the time you read this, you will be able to imbibe in their new bar and restaurant, located at 2700 Lake Street—still in the heart of the neighborhood most affected by the uprising. "It's very important to me that we have that space," says Montana. "It's a contact point for the community and we are dying to have that again."

The new space will have food to go along with the drinks, and he's hinting at a New Orleans-inflected menu. (He moved his family to the crescent city in 2020 and loves the flavors there.) Raising three Black sons, he had complicated feelings about staying in Minneapolis after 2020.

But it's Minneapolis that raised him, Minneapolis that supported him, and Minneapolis that made him, says Montana.

So a Minneapolis company Du Nord will always be.

THE WINSTON DUKE

DU NORD SOCIAL SPIRITS
2610 E 32ND ST., MINNEAPOLIS, MN 55406

N amed for Winston Duke, the first Global Ambassador for Partners in Health, a global health and social justice organization bringing medical care to under-resourced communities around the world.

GLASSWARE: Hot toddy mug

GARNISH: Cinnamon stick, pat of butter

- ¾ oz. Du Nord Mixed Blood Whiskey
- ¾ oz. Du Nord Pronounced Apple Liqueur
- 1 teaspoon brown sugar

1. Combine all of the ingredients in a glass mug.

2. Top with hot water and stir.

3. Garnish with a cinnamon stick and a pat of butter.

THE MARY JACKSON

DU NORD SOCIAL SPIRITS
2610 E 32ND ST., MINNEAPOLIS, MN 55406

Inspired by Mary Jackson, mathematician, aerospace engineer, and first African-American female engineer at NASA. She managed the women's program at NASA and spent her career helping to push women forward in the industry.

GLASSWARE: Lowball glass

GARNISH: Orange wedge, cherry

- 1 ½ oz. Du Nord Mixed Blood Whiskey
- ½ oz. Du Nord Cafe Frieda Coffee Liqueur
- ½ oz. maple syrup
- 2 dashes Angostura bitters

1. Combine ice, the whiskey, and coffee liqueur together.

2. Stir from bottom to top.

3. Add the syrup and bitters and stir.

4. Garnish with an orange wedge and a cherry.

STRIVE

DU NORD SOCIAL SPIRITS
2610 E 32ND ST., MINNEAPOLIS, MN 55406

Inspired by Mary Taris, educator and founder of Strive Publishing, who works to ensure diverse voices are heard. Her vision? "A world where Black narratives are centered, valued, and empowered for freedom, equity, and justice." This batch cocktail is meant to be shared with others.

GLASSWARE: Lowball glass

GARNISH: Cinnamon stick, orange slice, whole cranberries

- 1 (750 ml) bottle Du Nord Pronounced Apple Liqueur
- 12 oz. water
- 6 oz. Du Nord Mixed Blood Whiskey
- 1 orange, sliced thin
- 6 whole cloves
- 3 cinnamon sticks
- 5 allspice berries

1. Place all of the ingredients in a Crock-Pot.

2. Cook on low heat for a minimum of 3 hours.

3. Ladle the cocktail over ice.

4. Garnish with a cinnamon stick, orange slice, and cranberries.

YEAH YOU RIGHT

DU NORD SOCIAL SPIRITS
2610 E 32ND ST., MINNEAPOLIS, MN 55406

Yeah you right is a phrase that originated in New Orleans. Another way to say, "That's accurate"—only better.

GLASSWARE: Lowball glass

GARNISH: Dried or fresh apple slice, fresh thyme

- 4 oz. black tea, steeped and cooled
- 1 ½ oz. Du Nord Mixed Blood Whiskey
- ½ oz. Du Nord Pronounced Apple Liqueur
- ½ oz. brown sugar simple syrup
- 5 dashes bitters

1. Build all of the ingredients in a mixing tin over ice.

2. Stir.

3. Strain the cocktail into a lowball over ice.

THE MONICA HELMS

DU NORD SOCIAL SPIRITS
2610 E 32ND ST., MINNEAPOLIS, MN 55406

The Monica Helms is named for the US Navy veteran, advocate, and author who created the Transgender Pride Flag to lift up the community. She has spent her life elevating and advocating for others. Her original flag is on display at the Smithsonian Institution's National Museum of American History.

GLASSWARE: Coupe glass
GARNISH: Blue sugar

- 1 oz. Du Nord Prominence Gin
- ½ oz. Du Nord Pronounced Apple Liqueur
- ½ oz. Du Nord Mixed Blood Whiskey
- ½ oz. lemon juice
- ¼ oz. grenadine
- 1 egg white

1. Shake all of the ingredients together in a cocktail shaker.
2. Strain the drink into a coupe over crushed ice and garnish with blue sugar.

LAND OF MILK AND HONEYCRISP

DU NORD SOCIAL SPIRITS
2610 E 32ND ST., MINNEAPOLIS, MN 55406

Du Nord's home state is the birthplace of many famous apples—most notably the Honeycrisp. This drink brings out the best in Du Nord's Mixed Blood Blended Whiskey and the Pronounced Apple Liqueur.

GLASSWARE: Lowball glass

GARNISH: Cherries, lemon slice

- 1 oz. Du Nord Mixed Blood Whiskey
- 1 oz. Du Nord Pronounced Apple Liqueur
- 1 oz. nut or oat milk
- ¼ oz. simple syrup
- ¼ oz. lemon juice

1. Add all of the ingredients to a cocktail shaker.
2. Fill two-third of the way with ice cubes.
3. Shake for 15 seconds.
4. Double-strain into a lowball glass.
5. Garnish with cherries and a lemon slice.

THE BULLDOGGER

DU NORD SOCIAL SPIRITS
2610 E 32ND ST., MINNEAPOLIS, MN 55406

Named for the signature move of Bill Pickett, one of the most famous Black cowboys. His technique—grabbing the horns and biting the animal's lip—brought any steer to its knees. This drink uses honey to bring out the whiskey's sweetness, then adds delicate smoke with lapsang souchong tea. You can also use a coupe instead of the lowball.

GLASSWARE: Lowball glass
GARNISH: Lemon slice

- **2 oz. Du Nord Mixed Blood Whiskey**
- **½ oz. lemon juice**
- **½ oz. Bulldogger Syrup (see recipe)**

1. Combine all of the ingredients in a shaker.

2. Fill two-thirds of the way with ice cubes.

3. Shake for 15 seconds.

4. Double-strain the cocktail over a large ice cube into a lowball glass.

5. Garnish with a lemon slice.

BULLDOGGER SYRUP: Boil ⅓ cup water and pour over 1 teaspoon of lapsang souchong (or other black) tea in a mug or bowl. Steep the tea for 5 minutes. Strain the tea and stir in ⅓ cup honey. Refrigerate until ready to use.

EARL GILES DISTILLERY

1325 QUINCY ST. NE, MINNEAPOLIS, MN 55413

You're forgiven if your jaw drops upon walking into Earl Giles Distillery in Northeast Minneapolis. The expansive space is a stunner, with high ceilings, brightly colored murals, a variety of seating and a large collection of plants—more than 600, to be exact. But while Earl Giles provides a cool, comfortable place to have a cocktail or a wood-fired pizza—or to grab spirits, elixirs, syrups, or other cocktail accoutrements—what's happening behind the scenes is even more impressive.

The 18,000-square-foot space, a former carriage factory, is a one-stop shop for everything Earl Giles. "The distillery is 25 percent of what we do," says co-founder and partner Jesse Held. "We have a full-scale restaurant, a distillery, an event space, an apothecary flavor

lab, and a bottling facility that makes all of the nonalcoholic elixirs and syrups. It's the kind of place where if you can dream it, we can make it. It's all in one location." Earl Giles also houses an on-site mill, where they can mill and ferment whole grains for a true grain-to-bottle operation. Additionally, the flavor lab allows the team to experiment with more than 400 unique extracts and globally sourced flavors, then try them out in spirits and cocktails. Spirits, elixirs, syrups, and other products—even dried fruit wheels—are available in a small on-site market, while the ever-evolving cocktail menu is filled with products created just a few steps from where you're sitting. Talk about a green approach.

Held points to the Rabbit Kick as an example of Earl Giles's capabilities. "It brings all the elements of this whole building together. We're using extracts in it, we're using concentrates in it, we're using our gin. It's kind of like bringing all of the things together in this whole facility into this one thing."

RABBIT KICK

EARL GILES
1325 QUINCY ST. NE, MINNEAPOLIS, MN 55413

F̲ew cocktails are centralized around carrots or carrot juice. We wanted to lean into the uniqueness and the healthy qualities of carrots, says Earl Giles co-founder/partner Jesse Held. "Carrots have a natural sweetness and a freshness that is easy to work with when designing a beverage."

GLASSWARE: Lowball glass
GARNISH: Fresh-cracked peppercorns

- 1 ½ oz. Earl Giles Gin
- 1 oz. organic carrot juice
- ¾ oz. Earl Giles Lemon Citrate
- ¾ oz. vanilla bean syrup

1. Combine the gin, carrot juice, lemon citrate, and vanilla bean syrup in a shaking tin.

2. Add dense ice and shake vigorously until an ideal dilution and aeration has been achieved.

3. Double-strain the cocktail into a lowball glass over fresh ice.

4. Garnish with freshly cracked black peppercorns.

QUINCY COSMO

EARL GILES
1325 QUINCY ST. NE, MINNEAPOLIS, MN 55413

K eeping things simple and as close to the original design of cocktails is important—especially when dealing with an iconic and
popular cocktail like the Cosmopolitan, says Jesse Held. "We took the
original fabric of this cocktail—cranberry, lime, and orange—and
composed an all-in-one mixer. To create the vibrant hue, we steep
dried hibiscus flower, which also provides a subtle florality."

GLASSWARE: Stemmed cocktail glass
GARNISH: Earl Giles Citralia Cocktail Cologne, Earl Giles Silver Disco
Citrus lime wheel

- 2 oz. Earl Giles Vodka
- 1 ½ oz. On the Fly
  Cranberry-Hibiscus Elixir

1. Combine the vodka and elixir in a shaking tin.

2. Add dense ice and shake very vigorously. Proper dilution is the
magic in this cocktail.

3. Double-strain the cocktail into a stemmed cocktail glass.

4. Garnish with a couple spritzes of Citralia Cocktail Cologne.

5. Finish with a floating Silver Disco Citrus lime wheel.

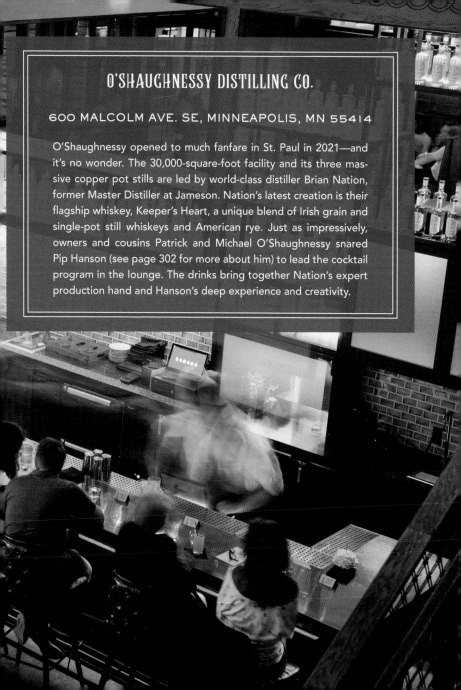

O'SHAUGHNESSY DISTILLING CO.

600 MALCOLM AVE. SE, MINNEAPOLIS, MN 55414

O'Shaughnessy opened to much fanfare in St. Paul in 2021—and it's no wonder. The 30,000-square-foot facility and its three massive copper pot stills are led by world-class distiller Brian Nation, former Master Distiller at Jameson. Nation's latest creation is their flagship whiskey, Keeper's Heart, a unique blend of Irish grain and single-pot still whiskeys and American rye. Just as impressively, owners and cousins Patrick and Michael O'Shaughnessy snared Pip Hanson (see page 302 for more about him) to lead the cocktail program in the lounge. The drinks bring together Nation's expert production hand and Hanson's deep experience and creativity.

HAYFIELD

O'SHAUGHNESSY DISTILLING CO.
600 MALCOLM AVE. SE, MINNEAPOLIS, MN 55414

The Hayfield is an Old Fashioned made with beeswax-infused Keeper's Heart Irish + American and salted honey syrup. The aromatics of the bitters and beeswax combine in an unexpectedly soft, floral way, while the salt cuts the natural sweetness of the honey.

GLASSWARE: Double old-fashioned glass

- **50 ml Beeswax-Washed Keeper's Heart Whiskey (see recipe)**
- **10 ml Salted Honey Syrup (see recipe)**
- **5 ml Demerara Syrup (see recipe)**
- **1.5 ml Peychaud's bitters**

1. Combine all of the ingredients in a cocktail shaker.

2. Stir with ice for 10 seconds.

3. Strain the cocktail into a double old-fashioned glass over a rock of ice.

BEESWAX-WASHED KEEPER'S HEART WHISKEY: Put 75 grams beeswax into a vacuum bag or Ziploc bag and add 1 bottle of Keeper's Heart Irish + American Whiskey. Hold the bag in a water bath at 167°F (75°C) for 2 hours. Place the bag in the freezer overnight, or until beeswax fully hardens. Strain the whiskey through a paper filter. Store it at room temperature; it will keep indefinitely.

SALTED HONEY SYRUP: Stir together 100 grams raw honey, 50 grams boiling or very hot water, and 3 grams kosher salt until the salt is dissolved and the honey is completely mixed with water.

DEMERARA SYRUP: Combine 100 grams demerara sugar with 100 grams water. Stir the ingredients together until sugar is dissolved.

KILLARNEY

O'SHAUGHNESSY DISTILLING CO.
600 MALCOLM AVE. SE, MINNEAPOLIS, MN 55414

T his complex sour drink harnesses the natural bitterness found in fresh radicchio leaves to provide a deep, herbal, amaro-like complexity. The bitter lettuce juice sour is more accessible and easy-drinking than it has any right to be.

GLASSWARE: Coupe glass
GARNISH: Single ice cube

- 50 ml Keeper's Heart Irish + Bourbon
- 40 ml Radicchio Sour (see recipe)

- 15 ml Rich Syrup (see recipe)
- 10 ml Cointreau

1. Add all of the ingredients to a shaker.

2. Shake with ice for at least 12 seconds, until the shaker frosts over.

3. Strain the cocktail into a coupe glass.

4. Garnish with a single cube of ice from the shaker.

RADICCHIO SOUR: Rough-chop 1 head of radicchio to fit into a juicer funnel. Add 150 ml lemon juice to the juicing vessel. Juice the radicchio and lemon juice, stopping when the total volume is 300 ml. Strain the sour through a paper filter and refrigerate for up to a week, or freeze for up to a month.

RICH SYRUP: Heat 200 ml granulated sugar and 100 ml water on the stove until the sugar is dissolved. Immediately remove the syrup from heat. Refrigerate it and it will keep for at least a month.

RED LOCKS IRISH WHISKEY

It's impossible to have a conversation about the Twin Cities cocktail scene without mentioning Kieran Folliard. The Irish-born restaurateur has been a fixture since opening his first spot in 1994, a downtown Irish bar called Kieran's. Since then, he's established several other Irish-inspired restaurants and bars—including The Local, The Liffey, and The Cooper—and created 2 Gingers Whiskey and The Food Building, a hyper-local artisan food hub that is a production site, market, and restaurant.

His latest endeavor? Red Locks Irish Whiskey. Created in conjunction with Powerscourt Distillery in Ireland, the award-winning blended whiskey is aged for four years in sherry, rye, bourbon, and virgin oak casks, resulting in a smooth, earthy flavor with a hint of vanilla. It's satisfying when sipped neat, on the rocks, or mixed into cocktails. Whatever Kieran's next move, it's sure to keep Minneapolis and St. Paul on the cocktail map.

IRISH 75

RED LOCKS IRISH WHISKEY

Marco Zappia of 3LECHE developed this whiskey-based version of a French 75.

GLASSWARE: Champagne flute or wine glass

GARNISH: Mint sprig

- 50 ml Red Locks Irish Whiskey
- 25 ml simple syrup (1:1 ratio)
- 25 ml lemon juice
- 100 ml sparkling wine or Champagne

1. Add the whiskey, lemon juice, and simple syrup to a cocktail shaker over ice.

2. Shake.

3. Strain the cocktail into a Champagne flute or wine glass.

4. Top with your favorite sparkling wine.

5. Garnish with a mint sprig.

IRISH COFFEE

RED LOCKS IRISH WHISKEY

Equal parts comforting and energizing, the coffee expertly pairs with the whiskey's rich toffee notes.

GLASSWARE: Irish coffee glass
GARNISH: Whipped cream

- **10 ml simple syrup (1:1 ratio)**
- **40 ml Red Locks Irish Whiskey**
- **100 ml hot coffee**

1. Pour the simple syrup and whiskey into an Irish coffee glass.

2. Top with the coffee.

3. Stir.

4. Top with whipped cream.

TATTERSALL DISTILLING

CENTRAL AVE. NE, MINNEAPOLIS, MN 55413

A leader in the modern distillery scene, Tattersall launched its Northeast Minneapolis distillery in 2015 and gained a quick following—and plenty of awards—for its craft spirits, industrial-chic cocktail room, and innovative environmental commitment. Though co-founders Dan Oskey and Jon Kreidler have moved operations across the border to Wisconsin (thanks to its more lenient liquor laws), the popular cocktail room still serves up drinks to adoring fans, who post up to sip creative cocktails crafted with house-made liqueurs, juices, syrups, and other ingredients. Here we speak with Dan Oskey.

Why did you start Tattersall?

For me, Tattersall is the amalgamation of a career in hospitality. I believe that flavor itself is an expression of hospitality, and the opportunity to create experiences through the language of flavor from the beginning—making a spirit—to the end product—the cocktail—was almost too good to be true when my business partner Jon Kreidler approached me with the idea.

What makes Tattersall spirits unique?

We don't settle on "good enough." We have to fall in love with what we're making, and we have to do it in a responsible manner. That bleeds into our commitment to being environmentally accountable. We have the largest rooftop solar array of any distillery in the country and have a one-of-a-kind water reclamation system so that no water from the distillation is wasted. Everything in our distilling process is upcycled, from the spent grains that become animal feed to the barrels, which become second-use barrels to age other spirits or are used in our restaurant to smoke meats and vegetables.

What's your approach to your cocktail menu?

We blend experimentation with what resonates with our guests. While we definitely don't want to be weird for the sake of being weird, we do want to create a moment of individual discovery. We construct our menus as a team, because palates are obviously different, and we see that as a strength. In the end, it's our goal to be approachable and accessible to any curious mind.

What makes the Twin Cities distillery scene special?

In one word: creativity. There are magical days here—such as today, where we got over a foot of snow—where chefs, bartenders, or creatives as a whole get some bonus time to experiment or put their ideas to the test. It wouldn't be so easy to do if it were 80 degrees outside with a beach down the road.

Where is your favorite place to have a drink/favorite drink to have when you're off the clock?

Stillwater Proper.

BONECRUSHER

TATTERSALL DISTILLING
1620 CENTRAL AVE. NE, MINNEAPOLIS, MN 55413

T attersall's recipe features aquavit, which adds a Scandinavian note to the classic tropical cocktail.

GLASSWARE: Lowball glass

GARNISH: Lime wheel

- 2 oz. Tattersall Toasted Coconut Aquavit
- ¾ oz. Matcha Syrup (see recipe)

- ¾ oz. pineapple juice
- ½ oz. lime juice

1. Combine all of the ingredients in a tin with ice.

2. Shake for 8 seconds.

3. Pour the cocktail into a lowball glass over ice rock.

4. Garnish with a lime wheel.

MATCHA SYRUP: In a saucepan, combine 1 cup water, 1 cup sugar, and 1 teaspoon matcha tea powder. Heat the mixture to a simmer on medium, stirring frequently. Remove it from heat and cool the syrup in an ice bath. Strain the syrup through cheesecloth.

UMEBOSHI SOUR

TATTERSALL DISTILLING
1620 CENTRAL AVE. NE, MINNEAPOLIS, MN 55413

A favorite since Tattersall's cocktail room's opening, this cocktail is well balanced with just the right tart notes, thanks to sour cherry liqueur and a dash of vinegar.

GLASSWARE: Lowball glass
GARNISH: Mint leaf

- 2 oz. Tattersall Rye Whiskey
- ½ oz. Tattersall Sour Cherry Liqueur
- ½ oz. simple syrup
- ½ oz. lemon juice
- 5 dashes black walnut bitters
- 3 drops umeboshi vinegar

1. Combine all of the ingredients in a tin with ice.

2. Shake for 8 seconds.

3. Pour the cocktail into a lowball glass over an ice rock.

4. Garnish with a mint leaf.

TWIN SPIRITS DISTILLERY

2931 CENTRAL AVE. NE, MINNEAPOLIS, MN 55418

Twin Spirits is the first one-woman-owned distillery in Minnesota. Founded by Michelle Winchester, Twin Spirits creations—including vodka, gin, rum, whiskey, and Mamma's Moonshine—are all made with unique ingredients or techniques, giving each spirit a special twist. The cocktail room is a perfect fit in artsy Northeast Minneapolis, with an industrial aesthetic accented by homey touches that give the space a comfortable vibe. We speak with Michelle Winchester here.

How would you characterize your spirits?

We try to create something unique and different in all our spirits. I didn't want to do the same thing as everyone else on the shelf. Our customers consistently give us feedback on how smooth and approachable our spirits are on their own.

What do your spirits bring to the industry that wasn't here before?

We use uncommon ingredients to create our spirits. We use cane sugar to make our M Vodka and M Gin, we use our own unique mix of botanicals in our M Gin, and we use a traditional molasses method for our M Rum. Our moonshine is made from Minnesota honey and only distilled on a full moon—that's unique as well.

How did you design the interior of your cocktail room?

I wanted to keep the space as raw and industrial as possible. We painted the ceiling a light blue to make you feel like you were outside. We brought in a beautiful mahogany bar that my brother-in-law created at his mill in Chicago, along with the mahogany glass-framed doors and window to let customers see the distillery up close. Then we tiled the walls of the distillery and bathrooms with white subway tile to give a clean and sophisticated feel. We really wanted to show off our beautiful custom-made copper stills.

What is your favorite Twin Spirits spirit?

The M Gin is my favorite. It has a milder juniper flavor than other gins. When giving tours, we always give samples of our M Vodka and M Gin, then let customers choose their third spirit to taste. Many customers have said they don't like gin. But I ask them to just try it as we get so many converts. I've never had anyone say they don't like it. It's always fun to watch a customer taste our M Gin and see the surprise on their face that they like it.

RUCKUS ROSEMARY

TWIN SPIRITS DISTILLERY
2931 CENTRAL AVE. NE, MINNEAPOLIS, MN 55418

Twin Spirits owner Michelle Winchester notes that they torch the rosemary sprig with a match or lighter in the winter to add a slight smokey taste.

GLASSWARE: Lowball glass

GARNISH: Rosemary sprig

- 1 ½ oz. M Vodka
- ¾ oz. lime juice
- ¾ oz. Rosemary Syrup (see recipe)

1. Add all of the ingredients into a shaker with a handful of ice.

2. Shake until chilled.

3. Pour all of the ingredients into a lowball glass.

4. Garnish with a sprig of rosemary.

ROSEMARY SYRUP: Heat 4 cups water with 2 oz. chopped rosemary sprigs. Heat the mixture until the water looks a little murky, then add 4 cups sugar and simmer until it's dissolved. Turn off the heat and let the syrup sit for 30 minutes. Strain and keep it in the refrigerator, where it will keep for 10 days.

SPICY TURMERIC GIMLET

TWIN SPIRITS DISTILLERY
2931 CENTRAL AVE. NE, MINNEAPOLIS, MN 55418

This Gimlet blends citrus flavors and mild heat with the slightly bitter taste of turmeric to create a well-balanced drink that hits all parts of the palate.

GLASSWARE: Coupe
GARNISH: Lime slice

- 2 oz. M Vodka Turmeric Infusion (see recipe)
- ¾ oz. Ginger Syrup (see recipe)
- ½ oz. lemon juice
- ½ oz. lime juice
- Dash cayenne powder

1. Combine all of the ingredients in a shaker with ice.

2. Shake until chilled.

3. Strain the cocktail into a coupe glass.

4. Garnish with lime.

M VODKA TURMERIC INFUSION: Combine 1 (750 ml) bottle M Vodka and 100 grams chopped turmeric (no need to peel, and the more finely chopped, the more turmeric flavor). Let the infusion sit, unrefrigerated, for 2 to 3 days, letting the vodka get darker. Strain the infusion and keep unrefrigerated.

GINGER SYRUP: Heat 4 oz. water with 4 oz. chopped ginger until the water looks a little murky. Add 4 oz. sugar and simmer until it's dissolved. Turn off the heat and let the syrup sit for 30 minutes. Strain and keep it in the refrigerator, where it will keep for 10 days.

THE INNOVATORS:

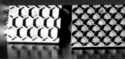

A LOOK AT THE PEOPLE WHO HAVE PUSHED THE
TWIN CITIES COCKTAIL SCENE TO THE NEXT
LEVEL—AND CONTINUE TO MOVE IT FORWARD

ANTHONY BRUTUS CASSIUS

3LECHE

ERIN FLAVIN

TRISH GAVIN

PIP HANSON

BENNETT JOHNSON

NICK KOSEVICH

MEGAN LUEDTKE

JESSI POLLAK

PEDER SCHWEIGERT

STERLING CLUB/BLACK
SOCIAL CLUBS

ADAM WITHERSPOON

W ithout the folks you'll meet in this chapter, we'd just be staring at a wall of bottles, dumbfounded and lost, tumbleweeds sorrowfully rolling down the bar. These are the artists, the craftspeople, the minds and hands that bring life to our favorite beverages in town.

Though this diverse group is doing wildly different things, collaboration is the common denominator between them all. The veterans who have made lasting impacts are still innovating as they mentor and inspire the new vanguard, and the younger phenoms are making their own marks, taking what they've learned and branching into exciting new territories.

In every case, these creative powerhouses are sharing ideas, pushing each other, talking shop, and collectively making our cities better and more exciting places to drink.

ANTHONY BRUTUS CASSIUS

When 13-year-old Anthony Brutus Cassius disembarked at St. Paul's Union Depot in 1922, he and his brother Benjamin made their way up Kellogg Boulevard Hill. They encountered a hotel, The Merchant, with a "Porter Wanted" sign in the window. Cassius went in to inquire. Even though the boss man told him he was too young, Cassius talked his way into the job. He knew there would be no record of his birth anyway—he was a Negro. Along with the job, he got a mattress in the basement to sleep on. Cassius lived that way, polishing spittoons and cleaning pay toilets and sleeping in the basement of the hotel, until he graduated high school.

The brothers were fleeing their birthplace on the rural outskirts of Tulsa, Oklahoma, known at the time as Black Wall Street—one of the country's most prosperous and thriving Black communities. It was not a coincidence that their arrival in St. Paul was the same year of the Tulsa race riots, one of the most infamous recorded incidents of white terrorism on Black people and communities in American history. In the aftermath of the destruction, about 190 businesses and over 1,200 homes had been burned down and destroyed—almost 1,400 Black spaces snuffed out overnight.

Cassius went on to become the first Black liquor license holder in Minneapolis, and the first Black person to own a bar in downtown Minneapolis. He remained in the liquor business for forty-seven consecutive years.

Minnesota doesn't think of itself as a historically segregated place—nothing so shameful as the Deep South, right? But racial covenants did the segregation work here in the north that Jim Crow achieved in the South. For example, Minneapolis law stipulated: "The said premises shall not at any time be sold, conveyed, leased, or sublet, or occupied by any person or persons who are not full bloods of the so-called Caucasian or White race."

Though racial property restrictions were prohibited by the Minnesota legislature in 1953, the resultant segregation patterns persist today.

Other practices deliberately restricted Black social spaces in Minnesota. For example, when applying for business licenses, prospective Black owners had to prove that their establishments would not be used for "immoral purposes." Additionally, local job opportunities for Black men were relegated to the ministry, the railroad, The Athletic Club, The Elks Club, and The Curtis Hotel. But of course, Black people working at the latter three would have been barred from eating, drinking, or socializing within the establishments where they served. Public spaces for Black people to simply exist were relegated to private homes and community centers like Phyllis Wheatley.

After high school, Cassius went on to work as a waiter at the Curtis Hotel, eventually organizing the first local Black waiters' union, resulting in a historic win of significant back wages and pay increases. A few years later, he went on to begin his storied four-decade career as a bar owner. When he finally opened his first downtown bar, in 1947—the

first Black owned bar in downtown Minneapolis—an article in the Spokesman Recorder reported that hundreds arrived and waited outside in hopes of gaining entrance.

By the time Cassius closed his bar for the last

time in 1980, his establishments had become known as the kind of place for everybody: Black clientele, yes, but also white cops, lawyers, and judges (thanks to the bar's proximity to the courthouse), local anchormen, personalities about town, as well as traveling musicians and performers. It was a good-vibes place where everybody knew they could have a good time with no trouble.

In an interview for the Minnesota Historical Society, Cassius said, "I had the pleasure of having a diversified business, where I always tried to see that people got along, and one of my criteria was that you had to respect the person next to you, and if you didn't do that, you didn't respect yourself. And on that premise alone, I remained in business for forty-seven years."

What we don't consider enough when we imagine bar spaces is the fluidity of their uses, of their necessity, of their inherent safety or potential dangers. White supremacy would have us believe that moving through space, in and out of it, whether private or public, is a no-brainer proposition. But that couldn't be further from the truth for non-white people. Cassius knew that. Because he was a Black man who created space for people to gather and just be, he was able to imagine a future that includes all of us.

3LECHE

THE FOOD BUILDING
1401 MARSHALL ST. NE, MINNEAPOLIS, MN 55413

Walking into the 3LECHE (pronounced "*tres leches*") lab space inside the Food Building in Northeast Minneapolis feels like stepping into a version of Willy Wonka's chocolate factory. But instead of Oompa-Loompas and psychedelic rides down a chocolate river, you're surrounded by a specially built sauna designed to heat a dizzying array of various herbs, plants, and botanicals at specific temperatures; expensive-looking lab equipment; and the warm, genial presence of Marco Zappia, one-third of the 3LECHE collective—no top hat, thankfully.

Zappia began his career at Eat Street Social—at the time the most influential bar in Minneapolis—under his mentor, Nick Kosevich. He partnered with Kosevich on his bitters company, Bittercube, and traveled on a punishing schedule, opening or consulting on several bar programs across the country in a short period of time. After burning out, Zappia stepped away and wrote a fifty-page manifesto on how the industry could evolve, attempting to deflate the tropes of singular genius in favor of a holistic view of service, teamwork, craft, and love. Zappia was then tapped to create the bar program at chef/owner Daniel del Prado's Martina, and once opened, the drinks exploded into the Twin Cities bar scene like a supernova.

Here's an example of a Zappia drink at Martina: Built in a spherical glass orb, it had stalactite-like spikes protruding outward from its exterior and a metal straw rising through a light fog that was somehow backlit. A crystal dangled from a fine chain, along with a small feather of uncertain avian provenance. The taste was a layering of flavor, contrast, sensation, temperature, and temporality. That *objet d'art* was both a fanciful, photo-ready gimmick, and a profoundly earnest offering of care and craft.

Such is the wizardry of Zappia and his partners Adam Witherspoon and Dustin Nguyen. As 3LECHE, the trio designed the original bar programs at several lauded Twin Cities restaurants and have consulted on others, introducing a philosophy and degree of thoughtful labor, prep, and craft previously unheard of but which is now becoming standard practice: fermenting all their own liqueurs and vermouths, making their own bitters, and now leading the way in developing culinarily complex nonalcoholic elixirs.

Since the pandemic, Zappia, Witherspoon, and Nguyen made a home for the 3LECHE incubator space inside the Food Building—itself a larger incubator for local makers using Minnesota-sourced ingredients to create products that have our particular terroir: Baker's Field Flour & Bread, Alemar Cheese, and Lowry Hill Meats.

"I think that next step is looking inward," says Zappia. "What can we make here that no one else in the world makes? What is exceptional about this place, instead of trying to 'Mr. Potato Head' things together, or regurgitate primary market stuff? How do we define ourselves and how do we lead and showcase the things we can all agree, under an inclusive banner, is 'us'?"

So what, in Zappia's mind, is representing Minnesota terroir in the cocktail space today?

"We're trying to define that right now, and it's not all on us—we're not operating in a vacuum. There are lots of other players at the table. The triangle between the University of Minnesota, producers and manufacturers, and the restaurant bar—solidifying that in a really thoughtful way is what we're trying to do. The points of that triangle are the Forever Green Initiative at the University, and they have two sections: one is scientists working on winter-hardy Minnesota perennials, and that's all they're doing. They're actively searching out the connections and relationships in the chef/bartender world, because they're not experts in the flavor category and they want to hybridize for flavor, not just yield. Then you have spaces like the Food Building. In the bartending community, that next wave of voices is coming up, and they'll be steering the ship, as they should be. I feel like we're at the precipice of a new dividing line—we're on the edge of that fourth-wave iteration of voices. What's a bar going to look like in a few years?"

As much as Zappia and 3LECHE are a closely knit clan of bartenders on the cutting edge of cocktail culture, they are philosophers, chemists, artists, botanists, and ardent care-givers. Welcome to their Renaissance.

ERIN FLAVIN

MARIGOLD
3506 NICOLLET AVE., MINNEAPOLIS, MN 55408

Erin Flavin had a rough go during the pandemic. As the owner of Honeycomb Salon in south Minneapolis, the hairstylist found herself without any customers—and thus zero income —when things shut down. "I experienced the pandemic in the same way everybody else in the world did, with all of the collective trauma-drama that went down with that," says Flavin. "Business shut down, and right when we were about to open up again after being closed for like three months, George Floyd was murdered and we boarded up."

Flavin found herself, like many of us, drinking more to cope. To survive as a salon with nobody coming in, she tried pivoting to selling more of her boutique hair products online. "But during all of that, I was in a drunken haze," says Flavin. "I decided that I could not drink anymore because everything seemed way more difficult. So I quit drinking, and a few weeks later my husband quit drinking, which is pretty awesome, because it's a really hard thing to do by yourself!"

At one point in her sobriety journey, Flavin found herself at the bar at Sooki & Mimi—chef/owner Ann Kim's Uptown restaurant—and tried their nonalcoholic flight.

"I was in this zone of questioning how to still be the person that I am, who appreciates music and art, food, and all the beautiful beverages that are out there," she says. "It was hard to figure out how I could still be me in that. Like, my dad owned a bar. I grew up with alcohol being the only way to socialize with people. I started researching what there was alternatively that would excite my palate the way that beautiful wine and cocktails do. Sooki & Mimi had just opened, and they were serving a flight of N/A beverages—and I was blown away. It was really cool to know that people were doing something like that."

Like many restaurants around town, Sooki & Mimi was utilizing some of the botanical nonalcoholic beverages made by local wizards 3LECHE. Founded by local star bartenders Marco Zappia, Dustin Nguyen, and Adam Witherspoon, it was and is an open-source beverage lab, incubator, and supplier of magical elixirs, both alcoholic and non.

Flavin initially had trouble finding them. "That was a real Zelda quest, man," she says, laughing. "When I finally found them, they just opened up their arms and took me in and it was like, oh my gosh. They're such cool people doing such cool things in this city. I feel very proud of what this city has to offer for nonalcoholic beverages and how far it's come."

As Flavin learned more about folks in the Twin Cities creating exciting N/A options, and with encouragement from friends and clients, she decided to start stocking them in her salon beside the hair products. She secured a loan from the SBA, and another loan from the Minneapolis Department of Community Planning & Economic Development, and was able to expand the salon's adjacent boutique space into a beautiful, bright, airy bottle shop called Marigold, stocking an incredible variety of nonalcoholic beverages—the first of its kind in the Twin Cities. And Marigold has been a massive hit.

"All of this helped me catapult this whole business into a reality that helped me see outside of being just a hairdresser. It's what everybody's known me as for the last twenty-some years. But with the N/A thing, I really felt like I found my inspiration in bringing this to people who are truly interested in having something wild to taste and be able to hone in on that piece that goes missing when you quit drinking alcohol."

TRISH GAVIN

EAT STREET CROSSING
2819 NICOLLET AVE., MINNEAPOLIS, MN 55408

Trish Gavin once broke a guy's arm with a bottle of Galliano.

"He pulled a knife on me!" she says. She cut her teeth at her uncle's South Side Chicago Irish whiskey bar starting at the age of 9 (according to Trish, he was an old country Irishman who thought everyone should be working forty hours by the time they were 6) and learned her trade the old fashioned way, by scrubbing out ice wells and bleaching grout. One day, a bartender didn't show up, and her uncle taught her how to pull a pint. That was pretty much it for her.

"School was the same thing every day—on repeat—but the bar was different every day. Different people having different kinds of days. I learned a ton about life talking to people. It was so fascinating hearing people's stories of the Amalfi Coast, Cuba, Ireland. I was hooked by the time I was 18."

Trish has come a long way from that "one-window Lysol-scented" haunt. She's headed up cocktail programs at some of the Twin Cities' most prestigious bars, most recently Khâluna, the Laotian stunner by Ann Ahmed that was designed to feel like a lush Bali resort. When Gavin started researching Bali, she found that the tropical island was rich with many things, but alcohol wasn't really one of them. So she traced the migration of alcohol to Bali and found that gin and rum came over on British ships, with the last port of call being Madeira, which she put on the menu. In line with its history, she made a cocktail lineup that's not "super proofy," infusing shochu, milk punch, and liqueurs, to name a few.

Gavin is also one of the first local mixologists to put a serious emphasis on the now (almost) conventional trend of nonalcoholic cocktails. "For a long time, we would get done with work and wonder how fast we could get hammered at the closest bar," Trish says. "But really what we're doing is unpacking what we've been packing in all night. We want to drop the stress and chill out for a minute. I think it's fine to have that opportunity, but maybe we aren't drinking consciously when we do. We should still have a way to destress, but not get hammered."

At her latest station, Eat Street Crossing, a global food hall on Nicollet Avenue, aka Eat Street, Minneapolis's food row, N/A options get as much consideration as the strong stuff. In fact, all of the drinks start out N/A on tap and can be mixed with alcohol upon request. They can also be made sugar free and diabetic-friendly. On top of that, a rotating list of charities benefit from what you can order at the bar.

Start searching out serious cocktail culture, and one thing starts to become glaringly clear: women, in 2023, are still conspicuously difficult to find. "If I had a dollar for every time a guy orders an Old Fashioned but then asks my [male] barback to make it instead," she laments.

Still, with garden variety sexism alive and well in the mixology world, she's behind the bar to stay. "It's a magical place—a meeting of the minds. A beautiful, mythical gathering where some of the greatest (and worst) ideas are born."

ARIES

EAT STREET CROSSING
2819 NICOLLET AVE., MINNEAPOLIS, MN 55408

Trish Gavin has named drinks after Zodiac signs at Eat Street Crossing. Cerebral and passionate Aries will love this meditation on chile pepper.

GLASSWARE: 8 oz. flared coupe glass
GARNISH: Dehydrated lime

- ¾ oz. fresh lime juice
- ½ oz. St. George Green Chile Vodka
- ½ oz. Tanteo Jalapeño Tequila
- ½ oz. Skaalvenn Habanero Rum
- ½ oz. honey syrup
- Pink peppercorn salt, for the rim

1. Add all of the ingredients to a cocktail tin.

2. Shake.

3. Double-strain the cocktail into a flared coupe glass that has a pink peppercorn salt rim.

AQUARIUS

EAT STREET CROSSING
2819 NICOLLET AVE., MINNEAPOLIS, MN 55408

With an Aquarian's penchant for water, this refrshing horchata-based dink is a fitting thirst quencher.

GLASSWARE: Fluted highball glass
GARNISH: Purple yam chip

- 3 oz. Ube Horchata (see recipe)
- 1 oz. Plantation 3 Stars Rum
- ½ oz. Clément Mahina Coco Liqueur
- ½ oz. Cachaça 51
- ½ oz. pineapple juice
- ¼ oz. fresh lime juice

1. Add all of the ingredients to a cocktail tin.

2. Shake.

3. Double-strain the cocktail into a fluted highball glass over ice and garnish with a purple yam chip.

Ube Horchata

- 1 cup cooked white rice
- 3 oz. ube, grated
- 1 cinnamon stick
- 1 green cardamom pod
- ½ oz. allspice berries
- Pinch freshly grated nutmeg
- 1 whole clove
- ½ whole star anise
- Sugar, to taste

1. Add all of the ingredients to a large pot or food container and cover with 1 quart of water.

2. Blend the ingredients with an immersion blender.

3. Allow the horchata to macerate for 24 hours.

4. Strain the horchata and add sugar to taste. This recipe makes about 1 quart.

PIP HANSON

O'SHAUGHNESSY DISTILLING CO.
600 MALCOLM AVE. SE, MINNEAPOLIS, MN 55414

"If I'm going to put a recipe in a Twin Cities cocktail book, I feel like the Oliveto should be it."

So speaketh Pip Hanson of his most infamous cocktail from the menu of the revolutionary—and dearly missed—Marvel Bar in Minneapolis. Hanson opened Marvel, the sexy subterranean lounge with a semi-secret door beneath sister restaurant The Bachelor Farmer, to great acclaim in 2011 (both businesses were sadly swept away in the wave of pandemic closings in 2020).

An emulsified sour using egg white and olive oil, the silky and meringue-like Oliveto required an intense shaking. As for how many Olivetos Hanson thinks he made during Marvel's nine-year run, he says, "God, you'd have to ask Schweigert!" [Peder Schweigert took over Marvel's top spot upon Hanson's exit in 2015; see page 328 for his interview].

Hanson came up in Minneapolis studying jazz drumming and barbacking at the Dakota Jazz Club under the legendary Johnny Michaels. "Johnny kind of birthed the Twin Cities cocktail scene with Tim Niver and Aaron Johnson [of Town Talk Diner]," says Hanson. "Johnny opened my eyes to the creative potential of cocktails. He made me see that there was an art form underneath the Sour Apple Pucker. He got me a job at La Belle Vie, which at the time [around 2005] was as good as it got for cocktails in the Twin Cities. I had my mind blown by the creative potential of drinks, and at the same time realized that

"If you're expressing the region you came from as purely as possible, nobody else can express it quite the same way."

maybe drumming music in general wasn't a viable career path."

Looking for inspiration, Hanson moved to Tokyo to study at Tender Bar with renowned bartender Kazuo Uyeda, innovator of the hard shake technique. "I ended up trading English lessons for bartending lessons in Ginza, and trying to learn all of their techniques. I came back to Minneapolis with the intention of putting those things into a bar. I met Eric Dayton [owner of Marvel Bar and Bachelor Farmer] in 2009, very shortly after getting back from Tokyo. I was 28, I started planning Marvel, and two years later, we opened it. And I did that for five years. That was, you know, a really special time."

With Marvel Bar, Hanson ushered an important new wave into Twin Cities cocktails, one based on intense technique and laser-like focus on the details—and proceeded to stack up all of the national accolades possible, including multiple James Beard nods.

"We built that program on what I saw in Tokyo," says Hanson. "I combined what I saw there with the new cocktail movement that was happening in the United States. We tried to fuse the two, and that involved a spare-no-expense philosophy when it came to perfection, and really doing things in the most painstaking way possible. That's kind of changed now. I don't know if I would ever do a hand-chipped ice program again, for example. I started realizing that there's more efficient ways of doing things. Marvel was kind of notorious for, on a good day, being fifteen minutes for a drink."

Post-Marvel, Hanson led the bar program for Artesian in London (considered one of the best bars in the world). Now, he's back. He built the bar program at the brand-new O'Shaughnessy Distilling Co.—a massive coup for owners and lifelong Minnesotans Patrick and Kelly O'Shaughnessy, who also lured former Jameson master distiller Brian Nation from Ireland.

"Ever since I was working in London, I've had an operational workflow that I thought would change the game in terms of speed of service. It took me a couple years to find the project to execute this, in terms of designing and building a whole bar from scratch. When I found it [at O'Shaughnessy], it turned out that their ambitions were

much, much bigger than just making cocktails faster. I had big dreams, but I never imagined it would be with talent of Brian's caliber. It's been a very special project."

Aside from Hanson's newfound playground, what does he see happening next for Twin Cities cocktails?

"An interesting thing happened maybe five or six years ago: it seemed like every bartender and chef I knew wanted to become a farmer," says Hanson. "Contrast that with ten years ago, when every bartender wanted to be a pickle-maker or something. You can really see the trend shift happen, and I think it's a positive one. The better the [ingredients], the better things we can make. Terroir is probably the most important concept in the food world since I've been involved in it. It's not just obeying seasonality. It's not just sustainable. It's originality, uniqueness, and innovation—and I would argue a competitive advantage. If you're expressing the region you came from as purely as possible, nobody else can express it quite the same way."

OLIVETO

MARVEL BAR

This was the most popular drink at the now-closed Marvel Bar.

GLASSWARE: Stemless wine glass

- 60 ml dry gin
- 25 ml lemon juice
- 15 ml extra-virgin olive oil
- 12 ml simple syrup (2:1)
- 12 ml Licor 43
- 1 whole egg white

1. Combine all of the ingredients in a shaker.

2. Add three cubes of ice.

3. Shake until the ice is almost gone.

4. Strain the cocktail into a stemless wine glass.

GATSBY

L ike F. Scott Fitzgerald's classic 1925 novel, this cocktail brings flashiness, decadence, and a bit of jazz all at once.

GLASSWARE: Burgundy stemmed wine glass

- **70 ml chilled distilled water**
- **50 ml Oban 14-Year-Old Single Malt Scotch**
- **10 ml Rothman & Winter Orchard Apricot Liqueur**
- **10 ml Bénédictine**
- **15 drops 3:1 saline solution (3 water, 1 saline)**

1. Combine all of the ingredients in a beaker.
2. Stir briefly.
3. Serve in a Burgundy stem.

MARVEL BAR

I t takes more than ten days to craft this cocktail—but it's well worth it.

GLASSWARE: Cocktail glass

- 1 liter Keeper's Heart Irish + Bourbon
- 600 ml Campari
- 400 ml Antica Formula
- 500 grams natural, non-chemical lump charcoal, broken into small chunks

1. Combine all of the ingredients in a large jar.

2. Let the mixture rest for 10 days.

3. Strain the liquid through coffee filters until it is free of sediment.

4. Rest the cocktail in a decanter overnight, allowing any remaining sediment to settle out.

5. Rack off the clear, silt-free cocktail.

6. Stir well with ice—a little longer than usual—and strain the cocktail into a cocktail glass.

BENNETT JOHNSON

LITTLE TIJUANA
17 E. 26TH ST., MINNEAPOLIS, MN 55408

You can't miss Bennett Johnson in a crowded room. He cuts a handsome profile—tall and slim, dark 'stache, long ponytail, a pair of Wranglers, and killer boots. He's been a fixture behind several important Minneapolis bars for years, getting his start as a barback at Café Maude on Loring Park in 2011 and touching down at vaunted spots like Hola Arepa, Tattersall Distilling, and Petite León.

These days, Johnson is co-owner of Little Tijuana, running the bar program out of what was, for decades, a beloved late-night neighborhood Mexican joint serving 3 a.m. nachos and oversized Margaritas. Johnson and his partners—Travis Serbus, Dan Manosack in the kitchen, and Ben Siers-Rients on ops—kept the original name and the yellowed awning, and they've got a double Margarita on the menu as a tip of the hat to the drunken spirit of the original haunt. But they tore out the carpet, brought in some analog vibes, and a serious skillset to the food and drinks, and today, Little T's is something truly special, if not rare: one of the best craft cocktail joints in town, yet humble.

"It's just unpretentious vibes," says Johnson. "But everything is dialed, you know, which is fun."

Prior to this new chapter as both owner and bartender, Johnson was perhaps best known for leading the team at the Tattersall Distilling cocktail lounge in Northeast Minneapolis, where cocktails were made with spirits that were being distilled on-site.

"Micro-distilleries were really new," Johnson says. "You can totally control the drink from grain to glass. I was excited about that philosophy. We were clarifying juices, we had a centrifuge, but we were also doing crazy volume. It was a really ambitious thing, but I learned a lot."

Just as the confluence of COVID-19 and the uprising after George Floyd's murder hit Minneapolis, Johnson became an outspoken voice for positive change in the industry, including leading a unionization attempt at Tattersall.

"It's in my bones," he says. "Both my parents were union for a long time. I've been around unions. I'm not saying every place needs a union, but I do like unions, and I think it was a valiant effort. And there was like a literal wave in Minneapolis after that in beverage. Now, as an employer and business co-owner—and I say this with respect or trepidation or whatever—but it put a lot of bosses on their heels, and rightly so, for some of them. It's like, do you have line people that are unpaid? I was hearing wild stuff from other restaurants, like, 'Show up three hours early and don't punch in.' What? That's crazy."

As a new owner, Johnson makes it a priority to listen to his people.

"I came up in the days where a lot of my bar managers were like, leave your shit at the door. When you come in here, you're at work and it's about professionalism, which I totally get, and I sort of agree with, but also like—are you okay? I ask my staff this a lot. Is everything all right? I want to know if they're good."

The consideration runs deep at Little T's, both on the menu and in the culture. When you're at the bar, you feel like you're hanging inside a warmly faded Polaroid. The minimalist DIY buildout suits the vibes, and maybe even dictated them a bit.

"If they would've said, 'You've got $3 million and unlimited time,' I would've been just spinning my wheels. I like having some guardrails," he says. "I like that it's an existing space—a very beloved shithole. Every day someone comes in and goes, 'I came here when in the 1990s, this was my fucking spot!' I'm just really stoked to be turning the corner of living in Minneapolis for twenty years, having this place now, and thinking about how I spent my late teens and twenties here. If you would've told 22-year-old me that I'd co-own the place someday, I would have told you you're fucking crazy!"

NICK KOSEVICH

The map of the Twin Cities cocktail galaxy would be woefully incomplete without the nebula that is Nick Kosevich. Since his formation at the long-gone but still legendary Town Talk Diner in the early 2000s, he's birthed dozens of stars that have gone on to shine brightly, many of them featured in this book.

Known for its boisterous and welcoming atmosphere, Town Talk was once an old diner on Lake Street in Minneapolis, and was revived by owners Tim Niver and Aaron Johnson. They retained the massive Vegas-style lightbulb signage out front, and brought in Kosevich. Kosevich brought playful and delicious cocktails to the Minneapolis masses in a way that hadn't yet been nearly as accessible—or as fun—and the place was an instant hit.

Kosevich moved to Milwaukee to start Bittercube, a company making high-end bitters from scratch and supplying them in bars all over the Midwest. Next, he returned to Minneapolis to lead the bar program at Eat Street Social, where every drink was built *à la minute*, and almost every element was house-made. It was always a party at Eat Street Social, with guests waiting dozens deep to guzzle their signature Of The Older Fashion, a take on the classic, and everyone drank a shot and yelled "SOCIAL!" when the bell behind the bar was rung.

"I think we were doing 25,000 Old Fashioneds a year," says Kosevich.

When Kosevich left Eat Street Social, he turned to a heavy consulting calendar, traveling North America training over 600 bartenders and helping to open more than sixty-five projects across the country. Recently, Kosevich created Drinks Apothecary—a custom cocktail ingredient flavor house—and partnered with Earl Giles to open their new distillery this past fall. As of now, Kosevich is a partner and the beverage director of Mr. Paul's Supper Club in Edina, Minnesota. In the Twin Cities, he also currently supports beverage programs at the

Malcolm Yards food hall, Can Can Wonderland, the Green Room, Getaway Motor Cafe, the Northeast Minneapolis vegan burger joint Francis, as well as the upcoming Gai Noi with Ann Ahmed.

"There's a collective, collaborative vibe at most places here in the Twin Cities," he says, "and there's a level of humility in our hospitality that is different than most places. If you think about places like New York, the population is so saturated that it's almost flipped, where it feels like, 'How lucky are you to be in our presence?' In the Twin Cities, it's the opposite; we still have to fight for every guest. The expectation is different from the consumer side, and my colleagues are excited to be sharing what they know with people."

As someone who has been deeply involved in the evolution of bartending here and around the country, Kosevich has a keen eye on what's happening now, as well as what the future of the Twin Cities cocktail scene looks like.

"I want to spray glitter and use flowers and have drinks floating in the air. Theatrics have to become bigger, because holding a jigger is not new anymore. Even bartenders think the use of these bar tools is archaic in some way, you know? I think it's really interesting, not only what our goals are behind the bar, but what the trends are and how they're changing from the consumer side as well."

MEGAN LUEDTKE

DDP RESTAURANT GROUP

As beverage director for DDP Restaurant Group—the empire created by talented local chef Daniel del Prado—Megan Luedtke is tasked with creating and overseeing cocktails for ten vastly different concepts (with more on the way). Her charges range from Oaxacan spot Colita to Italian restaurant Josefina to modern French restaurant Blondette to chic cocktail lounge Miaou Miaou. Whatever the menu, Megan and her team take a creative culinary approach to cocktails, using unique ingredients to create memorable drinks that make an impact for the flavor profiles as well as the visual elements.

What do you love about working with cocktails?

I love the endless ways to express a concept, a feeling, a time, a place, a flavor, a memory—really anything. There are so many new frontiers and things to explore, it's ever-changing and you will never know everything there is to know. They also taste good.

What is your approach to the many different DDP Restaurant Group venues?

Each place has its own concept and vibe. We look at a lot of history when concepting menus, whether that be Argentina, pre-Columbian Mexico, or France in the 1920s. Usually something will pop out at me and I kind of follow that thread to wherever it leads. Dani and I work really well together. He'll usually give me a few buzzwords and then we're on the same page, off and running.

Where do you find inspiration?

Movies, art, traveling, fashion, and visiting bars and restaurants. I love all of those things, and anything can really give inspiration. Tasting and learning about wine is something I go back to a lot when thinking about how to put a cocktail together.

What makes the Twin Cities cocktail scene unique?

I think there's a conception out there that we're flyover country and that we're behind the eight ball. I don't think this is true at all. There are people here in our community that are creating amazing things. Traveling to different places and going to bars that get a ton of recognition is great, but you kind of realize that we have a very cool thing happening here. Maybe people just need to catch up to us a bit.

What is your favorite place to drink when you're off the clock?

At home with a glass of wine, a gin Martini, or a Daiquiri.

MARAVILLA

It's crisp and clean with gentle waves of salinity throughout, says Megan Luedtke, beverage director for DDP Restaurant Group. "The botanicals of the bianco vermouth marry well with the brightness of the citrus and seagrass."

GLASSWARE: Collins glass

GARNISH: Seagrass

- 75 ml seltzer
- 40 ml Seagram's Extra Dry Gin
- 20 ml lime juice
- 20 ml shiso syrup
- 20 ml bianco vermouth
- 5 ml yuzu juice
- 4 drops MSG solution

1. Add all of the ingredients, except for the seltzer, to a cocktail tin and shake.

2. Add the seltzer.

3. Strain the cocktail into a collins glass over ice.

4. Garnish with seagrass.

MEKARUSHI

DDP RESTAURANT GROUP

The Cor Cor Okinawan rum was the jumping-off point for this cocktail, says Megan Luedtke. "I wanted to bolster the funkiness while not have it be overwhelming. I love using black lime, and combining it with the umami of the shio koji really makes this one hit all the right notes for me."

GLASSWARE: Lowball glass

- 45 ml light rum
- 25 ml black lime citrus syrup (with 3% shio koji)
- 20 ml lime juice
- 15 ml Cor Cor Red Okinawa Rum

1. Assemble all of the ingredients in a cocktail tin and shake.

2. Strain the cocktail into a lowball glass.

JESSI POLLAK

SPOON AND STABLE
211 N 1ST ST., MINNEAPOLIS, MN 55401

Many claim they are the best bartender. But only Jessi Pollak can prove it. She was named US Bartender of the Year in 2022 at the United States Bartenders' Guild's (USBG) annual competition—and that's just one of the many awards and accolades she's received for her work. As the bar manager at Spoon and Stable, Pollak has designed a bar program to complement chef Gavin Kaysen's fine dining menu of Midwestern classics. The drinks are elegant and fun, and expertly blend the familiar with the new—all while keeping sustainability at the forefront of what they do.

How would you describe your approach to cocktails?

At Spoon and Stable, we have intentionally chosen to couch our cocktail menu in the classics. For example, we use the template of a classic Old Fashioned, but with entirely different ingredients. Cocktails are hard to imagine for guests, so couching those things in the familiar allows our guests to have an idea of what they're going to receive, which can help guide them to something that they're going to prefer.

How does the cocktail menu complement the food at Spoon and Stable?

It mirrors our food menu in that everything is done with a lot of intentionality. Throughout both the food and beverage menus, we really focus on seasonal flavors and seasonal products—and we do it while reducing our carbon footprint.

What's one of the most important lessons you've learned?

Running a restaurant or a bar is absolutely a team sport. It has to be about fostering a healthy team environment where people want to come to work, work together, and do a good job. At the end of the day, our top priority has to be hospitality. You can't really do that alone.

What do you enjoy about creating cocktails?

I come from a fine arts background, and I absolutely love crafting drinks and creating recipes because it stimulates those same creative outlets for me. It's a visceral and satisfying process, but it's also low risk. On one hand, I might have spent six months on a painting in the past. But now I can whip up a cocktail, see if it's right, and then we try again.

Where's your favorite place to go during your off hours and what's your go-to drink?

I try to have balance in my life, so I don't go out to bars after I've worked. It can be a bad habit for bartenders because you need to de-compress, so I only go out on my off nights. I love the bar at Mara, it's a beautiful space. I also love Meteor. It's one of those places where you always feel at home right away, and you're always going to see some-one you recognize. My go-to drink is generally either a gin Martini or a scotch and soda. I like things nice and simple.

GIMLET

A precisely made, balanced, and complex version of the classic cocktail.

GLASSWARE: Nick & Nora glass, chilled

GARNISH: Dehydrated lime wheel

- 1 oz. Fords Gin
- ¾ oz. lime juice
- ¾ oz. Mixed Citrus Oleo (see recipe)

- ½ oz. Old Duff Blended Genever
- ¼ oz. Lustau Amontillado Los Arcos Sherry
- 1 dash Angostura bitters

1. Combine all of the ingredients in a shaker tin with ice.

2. Shake until well chilled.

3. Strain into a chilled Nick & Nora glass.

4. Garnish with a floating dehydrated lime wheel.

MIXED CITRUS OLEO: Combine mixed citrus scraps (the ends, peels, or husks after juicing from citrus fruits like oranges, lemons, and grapefruits) with an equal amount of white sugar by weight. Vacuum-seal the mixture in a plastic bag and allow it to macerate under refrigeration for 24 to 36 hours, massaging as needed to dissolve the sugar. Strain the oleo through a mesh tea strainer.

WHITE RUSSIAN

SPOON AND STABLE
211 N 1ST ST., MINNEAPOLIS, MN 55401

Proof that iconic cocktails can be improved upon, Pollak's version features Jägermeister and coffee liqueur for added depth, plus a cardamom cream topping you'll want to eat with a spoon.

GLASSWARE: Rocks glass
GARNISH: Cardamom Cream (see recipe)

- 1 oz. Tanqueray London Dry Gin
- ½ oz. Jägermeister
- ½ oz. Mr Black Cold Brew Coffee Liqueur
- ¼ oz. simple syrup

1. Combine all of the ingredients in a rocks glass with pebble ice.

2. Stir until well combined.

3. Garnish with Cardamom Cream.

CARDAMOM CREAM: In a stand mixer with a whisk attachment, whisk together 1 cup heavy cream, 1 heaping teaspoon ground cardamom, and 4 drops rose flower water until soft peaks form.

PEDER SCHWEIGERT

DRY WIT

As a bartender, Peder Schweigert's last official job was the equivalent of summiting Everest: he was general manager and spirits director at Minneapolis cocktail mecca Marvel Bar. He didn't know his nine-year run was about to end when Marvel Bar succumbed to pandemic-related closure, but Schweigert went out with a hell of a statement: his final menu debuted in January 2020, and he called it "Dry."

Dry was a menu of seven entirely spirit-free cocktails, largely comprised of foraged botanicals and fungi from the surrounding region, manipulated and massaged in the studied, cerebral way that Schweigert and the Marvel team approached their booze-fueled menus, and elevated into drinkable art. Simply put, the primary cocktail menu of the busiest, most famous cocktail bar in the city—and one of the most notable in the world—was going dry. This unheard-of move rocked the Twin Cities food and beverage scene. The excitement was palpable.

Fast-forward to today, a full pandemic later. Schweigert has developed and launched his new beverage company, Dry Wit, "a nonalcoholic blend of botanicals and verjus to be enjoyed with good food and even better company." It's uniquely delicious, culinarily complex, and packaged in beautiful 750 ml bottles that are fit for any type of table.

Having made the decision to stop drinking in 2016, Schweigert—an industry veteran who has worked with Dave Arnold in New York and Grant Achatz at Alinea in Chicago—has found the N/A space to be continually inspirational.

"What really got me jazzed up about doing nonalcoholic stuff is that I suddenly had this creative outlet where I personally benefited," he says. "And I got to see people—because there's so many reasons why people don't drink, right?—I got to see people suddenly connecting with the bar and the social space in a way that they thought was off-limits to them. Like, imagine if every bar in the country suddenly felt like a hostile place. So what gets me going is being able to connect with people, meet people where they're at, and make them feel like the hospitality experience is inclusive again."

With Dry Wit, Marigold, and 3LECHE leading the way—not to mention the proliferation of excellent N/A beers in our local breweries, largely due to the process developed by Minneapolis-based ABV Technology—the Twin Cities is a hotbed of N/A development.

"We're all friends here, and we support each other," says Schweigert. "Marigold's taken a leadership role in promoting it. We had a big event where we had a couple bands, a mix of THC and N/A, 3LECHE was there making drinks, and we were giving away tastes of Dry Wit. It was just a party, and it was banging! Two hundred and fifty people or so showed up."

And not a drop of booze in sight.

STERLING CLUB/BLACK SOCIAL CLUBS

Like most things in this country, drinking in a public space could not be taken for granted by Black Americans until after the civil rights movement. So, also like most things in this country, Black Americans had to take matters into their own hands.

The first Black liquor license holder in Minneapolis was a man who went by the name of Anthony Brutus Cassius, a civil rights leader in his time, and a man who endured a years-long battle to obtain his liquor license—a battle that, among other things, had him accused of communism by local government. Still, he fought for his license and won, going on to a forty-seven-year career as the first Black bar owner in downtown Minneapolis. His namesake series of bars, Cassius' Bar, provided crucial safe spaces for Black and white patrons who wanted a place to drink without suffering racism.

In the meantime, Black people in search of similar social space figured out workarounds. Social clubs such as the Credjafawn Club and the Sterling Club sprouted up, occupying private spaces such as party rooms in hotels (the Credjafawns were responsible for integrating some hotels and other facilities that refused to allow Black people the use of their spaces, by sending members of the club who were light enough to pass for white to negotiate contracts) and private homes, making it safer—if not necessarily completely safe—for Black people to gather, dance, socialize, and yes, drink.

Understanding that the needs of the Black community could not be left to outside hands, these social clubs also acted as food co-ops, credit unions, scholarship organizers and providers, and more.

Even today, there is a marked lack of Black-owned-and-operated food and drink businesses in the Twin Cities area, a direct legacy of the institutional racism practiced and exhibited by governmental agencies all over the United States.

Social entities like the Sterling Club—still functioning today—are understandably open only to members. But it is important to acknowledge their existence and the circumstances that continued—and in some cases continue to prevail— that make them necessary, and in fact crucial.

ADAM WITHERSPOON

3LECHE

Fortunately for us, Adam Witherspoon just sort of fell into the cocktail world. After working at Eat Street Social during its heyday, he interviewed to work with Nick Kosevich on his bitters line, BIttercube. "The energy, the excitement, the creativity—I needed to follow that somewhere," Adam says. While he never took a role with the line, it was there that he met Marco Zappia, fellow founder of cocktail collective 3LECHE (along with Dustin Nguyen). The rest, as they say, is found in the annals—and drinks—of Twin Cities cocktail culture.

Most recently, Witherspoon started the cocktail program at Four Seasons Hotel Minneapolis, crafting drinks for three different venues: Mediterranean restaurant Mara, Italian Riviera-themed Riva, and the Nordic Village winter oasis. Now, he is venturing out on his own, and we can't wait to see what he does next.

What's your cocktail philosophy?

Less is more. I love the creativity and the innovation that people are taking in the cocktail world. But there are a million gins out there, and I bet you like five of them are actually unique. Show me something new. Show me something that can stand on its own, and then let's pair it with something that lifts it up. It's like a relationship. You want somebody that's going to counterbalance you, but also prop you up at the same time.

If I add eight ingredients to something, then I'm shitting all over the work someone before me did. What can I do with three things that doesn't take away from any of those three things?

What makes the Twin Cities cocktail scene unique?

We have grit. There's a fine balance of big brother/little brother. Everyone wants to emulate the big brothers—New York, Chicago, Tokyo. But we're also far enough away from that where we still have retained a sense of individuality. We know who we are and what our community is about. I think that's where the grit lies. It's the combination of grit and isolation that allows us a freer playground. We're not super self-conscious, and concerned with, you know, do we fit?

What's your favorite cocktail?

Everybody hates it when I answer this question cause it's so specific. It's high noon on a blistering sunny day where you can like, hear the sun and the cicadas. I'm outside on the patio at Northeast Yacht Club [see page 345], and there's nobody there except one guy who keeps going in and out to smoke. I have a Tanqueray Tonic in a super flimsy plastic cup, with two little different-colored straws that are so small that you can't actually drink anything out of them because you squeezed a lime in and you mixed it up and the pulp is stuck in the straw. It's a perfect cocktail.

BICHROME MARTINI

This cocktail features a liqueur from the foothills of the eastern Italian Alps, called Kapriol," Adam Witherspoon says. "It's a single botanical distillate of alpine juniper. It's a beautiful expression of what juniper can be outside of just pine, with floral, fruity, herbaceous, and earthy expressions. The Bichrome Martini is the ultimate gateway Martini for someone who wants something softer and less singular than a Tanqueray Martini." For the vermouth, Witherspoon recommends either Yzaguirre Blanco Vermouth or Allora Secco Vermouth.

GLASSWARE: Nick & Nora glass, with a sidecar
GARNISH: 3 frozen purple grapes

- 50 ml Kapriol
- 50 ml secco vermouth

1. Build the cocktail in a stirring vessel.

2. Stir to proper dilution.

3. Pour the cocktail into a Nick & Nora over an ice shard.

4. Garnish with three frozen purple grapes in a sidecar.

CAPE TONIC

"The beauty in the G&T is that it is universal and can be ordered confidently anywhere in the world," Witherspoon says. "The Cape-Tonic is an answer to that. Caperitif brings new and fresh botanical structures to the forefront, and instead of a boreal forest in a glass we look to one of the most biodiverse regions of the world—South Africa—to provide us with bright, citrus-forward, terra-driven flavors with a production style—fortified and aromatized wine—with roots in the Mediterranean." Witherspoon makes rooibos tonic for this recipe, but Fever Tree makes a great and quaffable version.

GLASSWARE: Tall tumbler glass
GARNISH: 3 tattooed lime wedges, 2 pennycress sprigs, 1 statice sprig

- 50 ml Caperitif
- Tonic, to top

1. Build the cocktail in a tall tumbler over three to four ice shards.

2. Garnish with lime wedges, pennycress sprigs, and a statice sprig.

ICONIC DESTINATIONS AND LEGENDARY DIVE BARS

CC CLUB

GAY 90'S

MANCINI'S CHAR HOUSE

THE ST. PAUL HOTEL

NORTHEAST YACHT CLUB

331 CLUB

MAYSLACK'S

KNIGHT CAP LOUNGE

JIMMY'S BAR

GRUMPY'S

Drinking in the Twin Cities requires a stop at one of these legendary institutions.

CC CLUB

2600 LYNDALE AVE. S, MINNEAPOLIS, MN 55408

Usually the best dive bar is the one that's stumbling distance to your house, and while that may always be true, The CC is the dive bar that locals ask for by name. That's because this longtime establishment practically conceived of the iconic elements that make up a classic dive: well-worn pool tables, cushy yet tattered booths, take-no-mess servers, greasy meals, an excellent jukebox, a smoker's patio, and of course, stiff and affordable pours. Other things we like: the reliable lost-and-found box, where drinkers' errant scarves and hats go on to hopefully live another life; bathroom graffiti that pushes the boundaries of the artform; and the all-important fact that they are open 365 days of the year. This is ground zero for escaping your family on Christmas and tossing back a few with your chosen family of fellow drinkers. Stomping snow off your boots and settling into a booth here is basically a Minnesota induction ceremony.

GAY 90'S

As the name suggests, The 90's—as it's affectionately called by locals—is a beloved gay bar institution that is also on any to-visit list for a bachelorette bar crawl, 21st birthday, or simply if you need to shake your booty right down to the ground. It's far more than a bar. It's an annex to whatever you need at that moment: a dance club, strip club, kink club, drag show, low-key drinker's bar—the 90's has it all. Since 1948, this iconic building has been showcasing saucy entertainment, like strippers dancing to live jazz, and still today it's a refreshing reprieve from ever-encroaching downtown gentrification and hollow "concepts" designed by "brands" instead of barmen. The Gay 90's holds the not-so-dubious distinction of pouring the most booze inside of four walls locally, and once you sip, you'll see why.

MANCINI'S CHAR HOUSE

531 7TH ST. W, ST. PAUL, MN 55102

Think classic, and Mancini's Las Vegas Lounge is the place you're looking for. It's the spot all of those new retro, kitschy spots with the relish tray and brandy Old-Fashioneds are taking inspo from. Mancini's is the real deal.

Dating back to 1948, this St. Paul landmark has hardly changed a carpet fiber or an inch of vinyl on their circular red booths, situated for people-watching and liquor-sipping. It's a lounge in the truest sense: stay all night if you like, and nobody will be thrusting a bill at you and saying they need the table.

Live music on weekends is of the something-for-everyone, cover-tunes stripe, but the dancefloor, thick with booty shakers of all ages, is proof it's a formula that works. The adjacent steak house manages to stay affordable in the age of the $120 ribeye, with sour cream and butter pats still in their plastic bubbles, veggie sides that come in a medley, and foil-wrapped baked potatoes. Nobody is complaining about any of the above, especially if it keeps a properly cooked New York strip under $40.

Still family-owned after all these decades, you're likely to encounter more regulars than not, with multi-generational families comfortably holding down the booths—including kids bouncing back and forth at the edges. Mancini's hails from an era when a good time could be had by all, regardless of age or the size of your pay stub. Proletariat drinking places are becoming fewer and further between.

We'll raise a glass to Mancini's being around for another seventy-five years, and far beyond.

THE ST. PAUL HOTEL

350 MARKET ST., ST. PAUL, MN 55102

When you think of a Grande Dame hotel, this is it. Dating back to the late 1800s, with a storied history, The St. Paul Hotel embodies old-timey luxe, and is often the choice for visiting dignitaries, including none other than JFK, thanks in part to their perfect Martini. For $17, the St. Paul hotel boasts "generous portions," so it's a good thing the pillows to lay your head are right upstairs. Dusky mirrors reflect bottles lined from wall-to-wall and up to the ceiling, so there's no questioning what you're here for. Starch-shirted barmen are as proficient as they come, pouring a no-nonsense cocktail with the precision of the professionals they are. Pair it all with a bone-in ribeye and it's as classic an experience as you're likely to have in the Twin Cities or, well, anywhere. Its close proximity to one of prettiest parts of St. Paul—

Rice Park—means you can walk off the cocktail then go back for a nightcap. The Bold North Martini, made with aquavit, will warm you right up even in the darkest, dreariest days of winter.

NORTHEAST YACHT CLUB

801 MARSHALL ST. NE, MINNEAPOLIS, MN 55413

While technically a legendary Nordeast dive bar (see next story), it's situated off the beaten path enough to warrant its own writeup. Despite the name and the nearby Mississippi River, there's not a boat in sight—just regulars filtering into the squat, white, unassuming building, ready for a beer or cocktail, a comfortable conversation, and perhaps a game of pool in the rear room, which is lit up by neon beer signs. While the bar rings with energy on weekends, locals know that Northeast Yacht Club is the best spot in the neighborhood to catch a game. While not technically a sports bar, the TVs are always showing our beloved Timberwolves, Wild, Twins, or Gophers games—even the Minnesota State High School Hockey Tournament gets prime broadcast here—and you can count on a few fellow fans bellied up at the bar, ready to share deep knowledge, a hot take, or a celebratory toast when the game's going well—or commiserate over a game gone wrong. It's a place of cheap drinks, efficient bartenders, and an overall sense of community. We'll toast to that.

331 CLUB
331 13TH AVE. NE, MINNEAPOLIS, MN 55413

Start at the 331 Club, on the corner of University and 13th, and see who's on the bill. The anchor of the Northeast Arts District, the 331 has live music every night of the week, a killer lineup of excellent local tap beers, cheap domestic cans, and strong rail drinks. A generous happy hour runs from 1 to 6 p.m. with $3 pints. Every year in May, the asphalt parking lot becomes the musical epicenter of Art-A-Whirl, the largest art crawl in the country.

MAYSLACK'S
1428 4TH ST. NE, MINNEAPOLIS, MN 55413

One block over and two up, pop into Mayslack's, named for Nordeast native and founder Stashu Maslajek, a pro wrestler born in Minneapolis to Polish immigrants in 1911, who made his mark on the Midwest pro-wrestling circuit as "Handsome Stan" throughout the 1930s and 1940s. After his career in the ring, Stan returned to Nordeast and opened Mayslack's in 1955 with his wife Ann (who everyone called "Butch").

Stan and Butch brought in polka bands from the neighborhood, slung their famous roast beef sandwiches from the kitchen, and poured stiff drinks. Still beloved by the neighborhood today, the interior hasn't changed much—old-school charm remains, live music is a fixture, and the sandwiches are still massive, proving the rule that's eloquently laid out in a sign on the wall: "Nobody beats Mayslack's meat!"

KNIGHT CAP LOUNGE
1500 4TH ST. NE, MINNEAPOLIS, MN 55413

After all the beef, the only logical next step is to waddle across the street to the Knight Cap. They host a famous weekly meat raffle, a Minnesota tradition that's exactly what you think it is. Behind the bar is a massive tropical fish tank with iridescent species flitting back and forth while you catch flashes of conversations in thick Minnesotan accents. The smell of fryer oil floats through the bar, testing your paper-thin resolve not to order some mozzarella sticks, and coating the many large flatscreen TVs in a gauzy layer, lending all the games a blurry, dreamlike haze. Or is that just a result of the cheap drinks?

JIMMY'S BAR
1828 4TH ST. NE, MINNEAPOLIS, MN 55418

A few blocks north, the inviting glow of neon announces the warm confines of Jimmy's, one of the neighborhood's premier drinking institutions. Most Sunday mornings, Jimmy is known to bring in oily sacks full of White Castle sliders for whoever might already be bellying up to the bar, gratis. The pull tabs and Old Style flow freely, the jukebox is always playing "Black" by Pearl Jam for some reason, and you won't get away without hearing at least a half dozen of bartender Dave's dirty jokes. Order a shot of Polish (see page 352) and one of their homemade meat sticks, and you're in Nordeast dive bar heaven. As Dave would say after you order, "well why wouldn't ya?"

GRUMPY'S
2200 4TH ST. NE, MINNEAPOLIS, MN 55418

The final stop on the Nordeast dive tour is Grumpy's, or Grump's if you're familiar. All are welcome at Grumpy's, which they communicate via an ethics code intended to make everyone feel safe and secure. A slightly younger and hipper crowd keeps the Grumpy's patio lively, where American Spirit smokes go to die by the dozen, and the owners often fire up the grill for gratis happy hour grub on nice weather days. In the winter, weekly Hot Dish Happy Hour features paper bowls of their latest Crock-Pot concoction to warm your frostbitten soul, along with one of their vast selection of excellent (and rarer) local microbrews—with a bump, of course. A completely acceptable dinner any night of the week is a frozen Heggies pizza cooked to perfection behind the bar, served with an array of local hot sauces.

HOT DOG
WITH CHEESE & SALSA 300
350
HAM & CHEESE 500
ROAST BEEF 600

CHICKEN OR BEEF
TV DINNERS

SPECIAL SNACKS

LITTLE SMOKES 300
MICRO POPCORN 200

NACHO CHIPS
CHEESE OR SALSA 300
PEPPERS
NACHO PLATTER 500

PIZZAS

H

COMPLAINT
DEPARTMENT

BREW PUB
PIZZA

THE LOCAL FAVORITES:

WAXING POETIC ABOUT THE TWIN CITIES' ESSENTIAL COCKTAILS

THE GRAPE APE AT THE LOON CAFE

THE LOON CAFE
500 N 1ST AVE., MINNEAPOLIS, MN 55403

Minnesotans have a stark realization when they drink in another city and ask for a Grape Ape shot. "Huh?" the perplexed bartender will ask. Or else they'll make it, but it's a skeleton of the real deal, a randomly guessed blend of booze that happens to include Grape Pucker for the signature purple hue. It's a necessary lesson for locals to learn: One of our city's most iconic shots isn't universally beloved. Cue the record scratch.

Because, when made correctly, the Grape Ape is a bright, refreshing, sweet-and-sour pucker of a drink, a Kool-Aid-esque shot that blends equal parts citrus vodka and sour mix, and tops it with Buddy's Grape Soda. The Grape Ape is revelatory in its easy-drinking flavors (especially to a young drinker) and dangerously good (ditto). Many a local has found themselves at The Loon Cafe—a bustling, narrow, sports-y bar in Downtown Minneapolis—before a show at First Avenue or after a Twins or Timberwolves game or while bopping around the bars in the Warehouse District, ordering up a round of purple-hued shots to toast with friends. It's a rite of passage.

While other local spots accurately replicate the Grape Ape, nothing compares to The Loon Cafe's original version. It's nostalgia in a glass. It also offers another stark lesson: when you give in to the craving for another shot (and another, and another), the hangover is very real.

THE GREENIE AT TONY JAROS' RIVER GARDEN, NORTHEAST MINNEAPOLIS

TONY JAROS' RIVER GARDEN
2500 MARSHALL ST. NE, MINNEAPOLIS, MN 55418

Stepping into Tony Jaros' in Northeast Minneapolis feels like you've tumbled through a wormhole into a different era. A sign in the entryway reads TONY JAROS RIVER GARDEN PROUDLY TAKES GOOD OL' AMERICAN CASH ONLY!! You can almost smell the remnants of thick cigarette smoke, technically forbidden since 2007, still lurking in the ceiling tiles.

Not much has changed since the place was opened over fifty years ago by Tony Jaros—a professional basketball player who won two championships with the Minneapolis Lakers, and died in 1995—when he opened his namesake business on the corner of Marshall Street, overlooking the factories on the Mississippi River just north of downtown Minneapolis.

The Tony Jaros specialty is The Greenie, an ectoplasm-colored concoction of vodka, powdered Tom Collins mix, lime syrup, and soda over ice in a plastic cup. It's a legendarily potent cocktail that goes down like an illicit cup of Kool-Aid, and since its debut—which, as legend has it, was via the trunk of Tony's son Tommy's car at softball games before the bar was officially opened—it has developed a hardcore fanbase of enthusiasts.

On any given night you'll see the bartenders making dozens of Greenies at a time, lining up the cups in an assembly line, deftly tearing open the paper packets of Collins mix, and topping every glowing cup with a squirt of Sprite from the soda gun. While most of Tony Jaros' has stayed the same, they have expanded the original Greenie into a rainbow of hues—the Purple, Pinky, Brownie—you get the idea.

Is it good? Your mileage may vary. Is it bad? Depends on your expectations. Does it get the job done? Yes, indeed. The Greenie at Tony Jaros's is a required pit stop if you're hanging in Nordeast.

THE POLISH AT JIMMY'S BAR, NORTHEAST MINNEAPOLIS

JIMMY'S BAR
1828 4TH ST. NE, MINNEAPOLIS, MN 55418

Dave, the weeknight bartender at Jimmy's Bar—the platonic ideal of a dive bar in Northeast Minneapolis (or "Nordeast" if you're local)—follows up every pour of the infamous Polish with a rhetorical question: "How do they make it so good and sell it so cheap?"

No one seems to know the answer, and no one seems to care, as long as it stays that way.

The "recipe" couldn't be simpler:

1. Pour 2 oz. of Leroux Polish Blackberry Brandy into a shot glass.

2. Knock it back.

3. Cringe at one of Dave's famously bad jokes.

Nordeast is historically a working-class neighborhood with strong Eastern European roots—there's a bar and a Catholic church on almost every block. At Jimmy's, or any of the other excellent dives in the vicinity (Mayslack's, Knight Cap, Grumpy's, Shaw's, or Stanley's, to name a few), you'll likely see folks knocking back the strangely delicious, cough syrup–adjacent Polish.

After a few too many on a Saturday night, confession is just a block or two away the next morning.

REFERENT HORSERADISH VODKA AT MOSCOW ON THE HILL

MOSCOW ON THE HILL
371 SELBY AVE., ST. PAUL, MN 55102

An institution on Cathedral Hill in St. Paul since 1994, Moscow on the Hill is famous for having 300 house-infused vodkas on hand—the most famous of which is their Referent Horseradish Vodka, distilled at nearby 45th Parallel Distillery in New Richmond, Wisconsin. It elevates their Bloody Mary and Martini to enviable heights, but it's well appreciated on its own, served ice-cold in a shot glass with a sweet pickle garnish.

The vodka hits your palate colder than a gust of subzero air from a Minnesota winter, followed by a bold horseradish kick that clears your sinuses with a disturbingly pleasurable severity. The sweet pickle wraps it all up in a briny package that almost automatically requires an order of the excellent house-made pierogi for a savory, comforting balance.

THE VOLCANO AT HUNAN GARDEN

HUNAN GARDEN
380 CEDAR ST., ST. PAUL, MN 55101

If you have the dubious distinction of getting drunk for the first time on a concoction that arrives in a volcano-shaped bowl—complete with a burning lake of Bacardi 151 in the center—then we salute you. The Volcano is probably, almost always, a terrible idea. But it's bad in all the right ways. Hunan Garden is a dying breed of bar: low-lit and lowbrow, with greatest-hits Chinese food on the menu (think egg foo young and chow mein) and Polynesian drinks to wash it all down. This is the sort of place where absolutely nobody cares who you are, what you're wearing, or who you're with—refreshing, to say the least. Who knows what exactly goes into a Volcano, and why would you ask? Flaming cocktails are to drinking what one-night stands are to getting to know somebody. Here to get the job done—not too many questions asked.

THE WONDROUS PUNCH AT THE RED DRAGON

THE RED DRAGON
2116 LYNDALE AVE. S, MINNEAPOLIS, MN 55405

If you are a fan of an excellent dive, look no further. This type of windowless hang lets you get your drink on incognito with the regulars who seem to live on that same barstool, year after year. Hills of delightfully greasy fried rice, crisp fried chicken wings, and glossy chow mein provide the necessary base for the infamous Wondrous Punch, so named, in our opinion, for how you'll wonder in the morning exactly how you got so drunk on one drink. Served in what amounts to a fishbowl, this maraschino cherry–topped wonder is a concoction of many boozes and sugary punch, all amalgamated into a deceptively pretty peach color. But make no mistake—this cute concoction packs an incredible wallop. And please, you only need one. Scratch that—you don't even need one, but what's life without a little risk? "Wondrous" is just another word for astonishing. Prepare to be amazed.

ABOUT THE AUTHORS

Peter Sieve, Molly Each, and Mecca Bos are editors of *Meal Magazine* —a Minneapolis-based independent print mag that publishes diverse and compelling stories about people, through food.

Meal-magazine.com
Mollyeach.com
Bipocfoodways.org

ACKNOWLEDGMENTS

A lot of very busy people contributed their precious time and energy to helping us assemble this glimpse into our incredible cocktail scene. Thanks to all the bar/restaurant managers, bartenders, owners, and other people who contributed recipes and words. Thanks to Bennett Johnson, John Garland, Nick Fauchald, Joy Summers, and Geri Wolf for their guidance and expertise; thanks to A.B. Cassius for making it possible for Black people to have liquor licenses in Minneapolis; thanks to the McCabe-Johnstons for understanding why bar culture matters and fighting for it; thanks to Sean Sherman for featuring a BIPOC-only beer and wine program. Thanks to our loved ones for the support while writing this book, namely Emily Richardson, Sean Sherman, and Malachy Tobin.

And of course, thanks to the bartenders who remember our drinks, and have them ready for us when we belly up.

MEASUREMENT CONVERSIONS

	1 dash		0.625 ml
	1 teaspoon		5 ml
¼ oz.			7.5 ml
⅓ oz.	2 teaspoons		10 ml
½ oz.	3 teaspoons	1 tablespoon	15 ml
⅔ oz.	4 teaspoons		20 ml
¾ oz.			22.5 ml
1 oz.		2 tablespoons	30 ml
1 ½ oz.		3 tablespoons	45 ml
1 ¾ oz.			55.5 ml
2 oz.	4 tablespoons	¼ cup	60 ml
24 oz.		3 cups	750 ml

PHOTO CREDITS

Pages 6, 160–161, 228–229, 232, 233, 235, 236, 271, 272, 275 by The Restaurant Project; pages 8, 140–141 by Don Riddle/Four Seasons Hotel Minneapolis; pages 11, 147 by Adam Kennedy Photography; pages 18, 190–191, 192, 195 courtesy of Lexington Restaurant Group; page 19, 180–181, 183 courtesy of Can Can Wonderland; pages 20–21, 23, 282–283, 289, 290, 291 courtesy of 3LECHE; page 33 by Kevin Kramer; pages 41–42 by Mark Brown, Twin Town Media; pages 45, 47 by Steven Larson; pages 50, 53 courtesy of The Briar; page 55 by Laura Rae Photography; pages 57–58 66-67, 69, 71 by Travis Anderson Photography; pages 60–61, 63–64 by Anabel Johnson; pages 73, 75, 77 courtesy of The American Swedish Institute; page 79 courtesy of Francis; pages 81, 83–84 by Matt Lien; pages 86, 87, 89 courtesy of the Hewing Hotel; pages 91, 93 by Erik Westra; pages 95, 97, 98 courtesy of Lush Lounge & Theater; pages 100–101, 102, 103 courtesy of Manny's Steakhouse; pages 104–105, 106, 107 by Roy Son/Four Seasons Hotel Minneapolis; pages 108–109, 110, 113 courtesy of The Market at Malcom Yards; pages 115, 116 courtesy of Martina; pages 118, 119, 121, 122 by Jasha Johnson; page 125 by Heidi Ehalt; pages 127, 128 by Addison Avery; pages 130, 132, 133 by Annie Gruba; pages 134–135, 137, 138 by Jo Garrison; pages 142, 145, 332, 335, 336 courtesy of Four Seasons Hotel Minneapolis; pages 149, 151, 152 by Libby Anderson; page 154 by Victoria Campbell; page 155 courtesy of Terzo; pages 156, 159 by Michael Kyllo-Kittleson, Noselttik Creative; page 160 inset by Jill Hamilton; pages 163, 165 by Rachael Crew; pages 166, 168, 169 by Zophia Dadlez; pages 174, 175, 176, 179 by Alex Stahlmann; page 184 by Rozak Sowemimo; page 187 by Rebekah Poppen; page 196–197, 198, 201 courtesy of Pajarito; pages 206–207, 208, 211 courtesy of Baldamar; pages 213, 215 courtesy of Gianni's; page 217 courtesy of Getaway Motor Café; pages 218–219, 220, 223 courtesy of The Mudd Room; pages 224, 227 courtesy of Mr. Paul's Supper Club; pages 238, 239, 240, 242, 245, 246–247, 248, 251, 252 courtesy of Du Nord; pages 254–255, 257, 258 by Erin Dahlin Photography; pages 260–261, 263, 265, 304, 306, 309, 310 courtesy of O'Shaughnessy Distilling Co.; pages 266, 267, 269 courtesy of Red Locks Irish Whiskey Company; pages 277, 279, 281 by Connie Mrotek; pages 293, 294, 295 by Kadi Kaelin; pages 296, 298, 301 by Adam Klosterman; page 313 by Gene Pease; page 315 courtesy of Nick Kosevich; page 317 by Canary Gray; pages 319, 320 by Wing Ta; page 323, 325, 326 courtesy of Spoon and Stable; page 328 by Matthew Hintz; pages 348–349, 353 by Peter Sieve.

Pages 286, 287, 288 courtesy of the John F. Glanton Collection at the Hennepin County Library.

Page 330 courtesy of the Ramsey County Historical Society.

Pages 1, 3, 4–5, 12, 14–15, 16, 29, 34–35, 170–171, 202–203, 330–331, 338–339, 342 used under official license from Shutterstock.com.

INDEX

absinthe
  Corpse Reviver #2, 178
  Eat Street Social Naked Bal-
    lerina #2, 23
  Last Corpse, 199
  Naked Ballerina #2, 23
Acapulco, 162
Achatz, Grant, 329
Afternoons with Annie, 237
Afternoons with Annie Syrup,
  237
agave worm salt
  Morelos Sour, 65
Ahmed, Ann, 297, 315
All Eyez on Me, 48
All Saints, 38–43
All the Bitter New Orleans
  Bitters
  Natural K'Evan, 51
Allora Rosa Vermouth
  3LECHE Naked Ballerina
    #2, 26–28
allspice berries
  Strive, 244
  Ube Horchata, 301
amaro
  Bitter Butterfly, 168
  Machine Gun Kelly Manhat-
    tan, 221
  Manny's Manhattan, 103
  The Williamsburg, 193
Angonar
  Volstead's Old Fashioned,
    169
Angostura bitters
  Benny's Old Fashioned, 177
  Bonapera, 117
  Cold-Pleated Old Fashioned,
    234
  Gimlet, 324
  Manny's Old Fashioned, 102
  The Mary Jackson, 243
  Mr. Smooth, 68

Volstead's Old Fashioned,
  169
Angostura orange bitters
  Manny's Old Fashioned, 102
anise hyssop tea
  Madhaus, 107
anisette bitters
  3LECHE Naked Ballerina
    #2, 26–28
Anne with an E, 189
Antica Formula
  Lincoln County, 310
Aperol
  Bitter Butterfly, 168
apple brandy, about, 32
apple liqueur
  Land of Milk and Honey-
    crisp, 250
  The Monica Helms, 249
  Strive, 244
  The Winston Duke, 241
  Yeah You Right, 246
apricot liqueur
  Gatsby, 308
Aquarius, 300–301
aquavit
  Sazerac Thing, 91
  Schrutes and Ladders, 79
  Tattersall, 32
aquavit, dill-flavored/infused
  Aquavit Sidecar, 76
  The Huntress, 186
aquavit, toasted coconut
  Bonecrusher, 273
Argentine Sour, 111
Aries, 299
Arnold, Dave, 329
Arpece, 106
Averna Amaro
  Bitter Butterfly, 168

Back Bar, 164–165

Baldamar, 206–210
balsamic vinegar, apple
  Mango Shrub, 53
balsamic vinegar, white
  The Gibby, 39–40
  The Huntress, 186
Bartlett, Marley, 167, 169
Basement Bar, 162
Bashkodejiibik, 129
Beavers, Torrance, 174
Bee Pollen-Honey Syrup
  God Save the Queen, 120
  recipe, 120
Beer Back, Shot and a, 132
Beeswax-Washed Keeper's
  Heart Whiskey
  Hayfield, 262–263
  recipe, 262
beet and carrot juice
  Schrutes and Ladders, 79
Bénédictine
  All Eyez on Me, 48
  Gatsby, 308
Benny's Old Fashioned, 177
bergamot, dried
  Bashkodejiibik, 129
berry ratafia
  Madhaus, 107
Bichrome Martini, 334
Billy Sushi/Billy After Dark,
  44–48
bitter almond ratafia
  Arpece, 106
Bitter Butterfly, 168
Bittercube, 332
Bittercube Blackstrap Bitters
  The Northern Way, 112
Bittercube Trinity Bitters
  Hewing Old Fashioned, 87
Bittermens Hellfire Shrub
  Bitters

Reel-to-Reel Sling, 164–165
bitters
Yeah You Right, 246
see also individual bitters
black lime citrus syrup
Mekarushi, 321
Black social clubs, 330
black walnut bitters
Umeboshi Sour, 274
blackberries
Afternoons with Annie
Syrup, 237
Bashkodejiibik, 129
Bonapera, 117
Bonecrusher, 273
Bordiga Aperitivo
Nebbia Rosa, 157
Bos, Mecca, 37, 173
bourbon
Bitter Butterfly, 168
Bourbon Street Smash, 70
Hewing Old Fashioned, 87
Honey Badger, 88
Hot Rush, 153
Killarney, 264–265
Lincoln County, 310
Morelos Sour, 65
Mr. Smooth, 68
N.Y.F.O.F. (Not Your Father's
Old Fashioned), 209
Reel-to-Reel Sling, 164–165
Volstead's Old Fashioned,
169
Bradstreet Crafthouse, 18
brandy
Bonapera, 117
brandy, apple, about, 32
brandy, blackberry
The Polish, 352
Braulio
Nebbia Rosa, 157
Bresca Dorada Mirto
Sardinian Spritz, 158
Briar, The, 49–53
Broder family, 154–155
Brother Justus Whiskey Com-
pany, 232–237
brown sugar simple syrup
Yeah You Right, 246
brown sugar sour
Bourbon Street Smash, 70
Brunson's Pub, 174–178
Brut Cava
All Eyez on Me, 48

Bubble Gum Air, 182
Bubble Up, 182
Bulldogger, The, 253
Bulldogger Syrup, 253
Cachaça 51
Aquarius, 300–301
Café & Bar Lurcat, 54–59
Cafe Maude, 18
Campari
Grapefruit Negroni, 194
Lincoln County, 310
Can Can Wonderland, 181–
182, 315
Cape Tonic, 337
Caperitif
Cape Tonic, 337
Cappelletti Aperitivo
Crystal Palace, 143
cardamom bitters
Sardinian Spritz, 158
Cardamom Cream
recipe, 327
White Russian, 327
cardamom pods
Ube Horchata, 301
White Wine Glögg, 74–75
carrot juice
14 Karrot Queen, 210
Rabbit Kick, 256
Schrutes and Ladders, 79
Young Buck Mix, 43
Cassius, Anthony Brutus, 10,
286–288, 330
CC Club, 341
Centro, 61–65
Champagne
Irish 75, 268
Lush 75, 268
Champagne vinegar
Mango Shrub, 53
charcoal
Lincoln County, 310
Charred Scallion Dry Ver-
mouth
The Gibby, 39–40
recipe, 40
Chartreuse, green
Anne with an E, 189
Last Corpse, 199
Chartreuse, yellow
Honey Badger, 88
cherry bark/vanilla bitters
N.Y.F.O.F. (Not Your Father's

Old Fashioned), 209
cherry juice
Machine Gun Kelly Manhat-
tan, 221
Chile–Infused Mezcal, Tama-
rind and Thai, 85
Chino Latino, 17
chipotle sour
Morelos Sour, 65
Chupacabra, 123
Cilantro Margarita, Habanero,
200–201
cinchona bark
Manoomin, 126
cinnamon sticks
Strive, 244
Ube Horchata, 301
White Wine Glögg, 74–75
citric and malic acid solution
Arpece, 106
citrus
Dunbar's Numbers, 139
Clément Mahina Coco Li-
queur
Aquarius, 300–301
cloves
Strive, 244
Ube Horchata, 301
White Wine Glögg, 74–75
Cocchi Americano
Corpse Reviver #2, 178
Last Corpse, 199
Cocchi Americano Bianco
God Save the Queen, 120
Cocchi Americano Rosa
Naked Ballerina #2, 23
cocoa bitters
The Williamsburg, 193
coconut cream
Piña Colada, 92
coffee
Afternoons with Annie, 237
Irish Coffee, 269
see also espresso
coffee, hazelnut-infused
Espresso Martini, 96
coffee liqueur
Espresso Martini, 59
Martini Espress, 149
The Mary Jackson, 243
Orange Moon, 144
White Russian, 327
cognac
All Eyez on Me, 48

Mr. Paul's Supper Club
  Sazerac, 225
Mr. Smooth, 68
Cointreau
  Killarney, 264–265
Cold-Pleated Old Fashioned, 234
Corpse Reviver #2, 178
cranberries
  Bashkodejiibik, 129
cranberry juice
  Soul of the City, 222
cranberry liqueur
  Soul of the City, 222
cranberry-hibiscus elixir
  Quincy Cosmo, 259
Credjafawn Club, 330
Cry Baby Craig's Hot Honey
  Hot Rush, 153
Crystal Palace, 143
curaçao, dry
  Anne with an E, 189
curaçao, orange
  Habanero Cilantro Margarita, 200–201
Cynar
  Mr. Smooth, 68
  Piña Colada, 92
  Volstead's Old Fashioned, 169

Dakota, The, 66–70
Dale DeGroff Daiquiri, 17
Dashfire bitters, about, 32
Dayton, Eric, 303
DDP Restaurant Group, 316–321
del Prado, Danny, 114, 289, 316
Demerara Syrup
  Bonapera, 117
  Hayfield, 262–263
  Manny's Old Fashioned, 102
  recipe, 263
  Volstead's Old Fashioned, 169
Dirty Martini, 214
Don't Sweat the Technique, 46
Dreamsicle, 150
Drinks Apothecary, 314
Dry Wit, 33, 328–329
Du Nord Social Spirits, 10, 238–253
Dunbar's Numbers, 139

Dusty's Northeast, 119
Each, Molly, 205
Earl Giles Distillery, 254–259, 314
Earl Giles syrups and elixirs
  about, 32
  Argentine Sour, 111
  Hurricane, 226
  Matcha Gimlet, 216
  Rabbit Kick, 256
  Schrutes and Ladders, 79
Earl Grey tea
  Madhaus, 107
Eat Street Crossing, 296–301
Eat Street Social, 19, 22, 314
Eat Street Social Naked Ballerina #2, 23
eggs/egg whites
  Anne with an E, 189
  Dreamsicle, 150
  14 Karrot Queen, 210
  The Monica Helms, 249
  Oliveto, 307
  Soul of the City, 222
Emerald Lounge, 185–189
epazote simple syrup
  Sazerac Thing, 91
espresso
  Espresso Martini, 96
  Martini Espress, 149
  see also coffee

fennel bittered piloncillo
  syrup
  Mr. Paul's Supper Club
    Sazerac, 225
fernet
  Argentine Sour, 111
Fika, 72–76
Filthy Cherry Juice
  Machine Gun Kelly Manhattan, 221
Flavin, Erin, 9, 292–295
Floyd, George, 9, 238
Folliard, Kieran, 266
Four Seasons Hotel Minneapolis, 332, 334, 337
14 Karrot Queen, 210
Francis, 78–79
Frangelico
  Espresso Martini, 59
Frozen Vodka Martini, 136

Gatsby, 308

Gavin, Trish, 18, 296–297, 299
Gay 90's, 343
Genever
  Gimlet, 324
Getaway Motor Cafe, 216
Gianni's Steakhouse, 212, 214
Gibby, The, 39–40
Gimlet, 324
gin
  about, 32
  Anne with an E, 189
  Arpece, 106
  Corpse Reviver #2, 178
  Dirty Martini, 214
  Dreamsicle, 150
  14 Karrot Queen, 210
  The Gibby, 39–40
  Gimlet, 324
  God Save the Queen, 120
  Grapefruit Negroni, 194
  The Huntress, 186
  Madhaus, 107
  Maravilla, 318
  The Monica Helms, 249
  Oliveto, 307
  Petit Jolie l'Orange, 56
  Rabbit Kick, 256
  White Russian, 327
ginger, fresh
  White Wine Glögg, 74–75
ginger, wild
  Bashkodejiibik, 129
ginger juice
  Young Buck Mix, 43
ginger lemon honey elixir
  The Northern Way, 112
ginger liqueur
  14 Karrot Queen, 210
ginger simple syrup
  Bitter Butterfly, 168
Ginger Syrup
  Honey Badger, 88
  Next Up . . ., 82–83
  recipe, 83, 88, 281
  Reel-to-Reel Sling, 164–165
  Spicy Turmeric Gimlet, 280–281
God Save the Queen, 120
Goldenrod, Evan, 49
Grain Belt Premium, about, 33
Grape Ape, The, 350
grapefruit juice
  Acapulco, 162

The Palmloma, 133
grapefruit lime elixir
  Argentine Sour, 111
  Schrutes and Ladders, 79
Grapefruit Negroni, 194
grapefruit peels
  Anne with an E, 189
grappa
  Bonapera, 117
Greenie, The, 351
grenadine
  The Monica Helms, 249
Grumpy's, 347

Habanero Cilantro Margarita,
  200–201
Habanero Tincture
  Habanero Cilantro Margar-
    ita, 200–201
  recipe, 201
Hai Hai, 80–85
Hamm's Beer, about, 33
Hanson, Pip, 11–12, 18, 302–
  305
hawthorne berry
  Manoomin, 126
Hayfield, 262–263
hazelnut liqueur
  Espresso Martini, 59
Heidi's, 18
Held, Jesse, 19, 254–255, 256,
  259
hemp milk
  Manoomin, 126
Hennessy, Paul, 104
Hewing Bar & Lounge and
  Tullibee Restaurant, 86–88
Hewing Old Fashioned, 87
hibiscus flowers, dried
  Tropical Tea, 52
hibiscus ginger kombucha
  Reel-to-Reel Sling, 164–165
hibiscus tea
  Dunbar's Numbers, 139
honey
  God Save the Queen, 120
  Honey Badger, 88
  Hot Rush, 153
  Salted Honey Syrup, 263
honey syrup
  Anne with an E, 189
  Aries, 299

Hot Rush, 153
Hunan Garden, 354–355
Huntress, The, 186
Hurricane, 226

Irish 75, 268
Irish Coffee, 269
Italicus Bergamotto
  Petit Jolie l'Orange, 56

Jackson, Mary, 206
Jägermeister
  White Russian, 327
Jamaican #1 Bitters
  Naked Ballerina #2, 23
Jimmy's Bar, 347, 352
Johnson, Aaron, 314
Johnson, Bennett, 90, 311–
  312
Johnson, Ole, 54
Johnson, Patrice, 76
Johnston, Jasha, 118–119

Kapriol
  Bichrome Martini, 334
Kaysesn, Gavin, 104
Khâluna, 297
Kieck, Kenneth, 206
Killarney, 264–265
Kim, Ann, 160, 292
Knight Cap Lounge, 346–347
kombucha vinegar
  Mango Shrub, 53
Kosevich, Nick, 17, 78, 108,
  111, 216, 289, 314–315, 332
Kreidler, Jon, 270
Kupitz, Ross, 54–55

La Belle Vie, 18
La Luna Cupreata
  Last Corpse, 199
LaFleche, Thomas and Molly,
  174
Land of Milk and Honeycrisp,
  250
Last Corpse, 199
lemongrass-rose syrup
  Arpece, 106
lemons/lemon juice
  Afternoons with Annie, 237
  All Eyez on Me, 48
  Anne with an E, 189

Aquavit Sidecar, 76
Bitter Butterfly, 168
The Bulldogger, 253
Corpse Reviver #2, 178
Don't Sweat the Technique,
  46
God Save the Queen, 120
Hot Rush, 153
Irish 75, 268
Land of Milk and Honey-
  crisp, 250
Martina Naked Ballerina #2,
  24–26
The Monica Helms, 249
Morelos Sour, 65
Naked Ballerina #2, 23
Nebbia Rosa, 157
Oliveto, 307
Radicchio Sour, 264
Sardinian Spritz, 158
Spicy Turmeric Gimlet,
  280–281
Umeboshi Sour, 274
Lexington, The, 190–194
Liay, Mike, 135
Licor 43
  Oliveto, 307
licorice root
  Tropical Tea, 52
lime elixir
  Matcha Gimlet, 216
limes/lime juice
  Aquarius, 300–301
  Aries, 299
  Bonecrusher, 273
  Gimlet, 324
  Habanero Cilantro Margar-
    ita, 200–201
  Honey Badger, 88
  Last Corpse, 199
  Maravilla, 318
  Mekarushi, 321
  Next Up . . ., 82–83
  The Palmloma, 133
  Piña Colada, 92
  Pineapple Passion Daiquiri,
    212
  Postcards from Palawan, 85
  Quincy Margarita, 62
  Reel-to-Reel Sling, 164–165
  Ruckus Rosemary, 278
  Soul of the City, 222
  Spicy Turmeric Gimlet,
    280–281

Lincoln County, 310

Liquor Lyle's, 119

Little Tijuana, 90–92, 311–312

Loon Cafe, The, 350

Lovejoy's Bloody Mary Mix, about, 32

Luedtke, Megan, 316–321

Luesse, Adam, 114

Lush 75, 99

Lush Lounge & Theater, 94–99

lychee liqueur
Dunbar's Numbers, 139

M Vodka Turmeric Infusion
recipe, 280
Spicy Turmeric Gimlet, 280–281

Machine Gun Kelly Manhattan, 221

Madhaus, 107

Maeyaeret, Elle, 66

Mancini's Char House, 343–344

Mango Shrub
recipe, 53
Tropicalía, 52–53

Manny's Manhattan, 103

Manny's Old Fashioned, 102

Manny's Steakhouse, 100–103

Manoomin, 126

Manosack, Dan, 90, 311

maple sarsaparilla tea
Manoomin, 126

maple syrup
The Mary Jackson, 243
Natural K'Evan, 51

Mara Restaurant & Bar, 104–107

Maravilla, 318

Marigold, 9, 292–295, 329

Market at Malcolm Yards, The, 108–112

Martina, 24–26, 114–116

Martina Naked Ballerina #2, 24–26

Martini Espress, 149

Marvel Bar, 10, 18, 302, 303, 307–309, 328

Mary Jackson, The, 243

Matcha Gimlet, 216

Matcha Syrup

Bonecrusher, 273
recipe, 273

maté
Argentine Sour, 111

Mayslack's, 346

McCabe-Johnston, Carrie, 118–119

McCabe-Johnston, Jakob, 123

measurement conversions, 358

Mekarushi, 321

Merrill, Sean, 206

methylcellulose
Schrutes and Ladders, 79

mezcal
Postcards from Palawan, 85
Tamarind and Thai Chile–Infused Mezcal, 85
see also tequila

Michaels, Johnny, 18, 302

milk, nut or oat
Land of Milk and Honeycrisp, 250

mint leaves
Afternoons with Annie Syrup, 237
Bourbon Street Smash, 70

Mixed Citrus Oleo Gimlet, 324
recipe, 324

mizu green tea
Don't Sweat the Technique, 46

mole bitters
Sazerac Thing, 91

Monica Helms, The, 249

Montana, Chris, 10, 238–239

Morelos Sour, 65

Mortimer's, 119

Moscow on the Hill, 354

Mr. Paul's Supper Club, 225–226, 314

Mr. Paul's Supper Club Sazerac, 225

Mr. Smooth, 68

MSG solution
Maravilla, 318

Mudd Room, The, 219–222

mugolio
Natural K'Evan, 51

N/A cocktails
about, 9
Bashkodejibik, 129

Flavin and, 292, 294–295
Gavin and, 297
Manoomin, 126
Natural K'Evan, 51
Schweigert and, 329
Tropicalía, 52–53
Young Buck, 43

Naked Ballerina, 22

Naked Ballerina #2, 22–23

Nation, Brian, 12, 261, 303, 305

Natural K'Evan, 51

Nebbia Rosa, 157

nettle, dried
Bashkodejiibik, 129

Next Up . . ., 82–83

Nguyen, Christina, 80–81

Nguyen, Dustin, 290, 294, 332

Nightingale, 118–123

Niver, Tim, 17, 314

North Star Cocktails (Michaels), 18

Northeast Yacht Club, 345

Northern Way, The, 112

nutmeg
Ube Horchata, 301

N.Y.F.O.F. (Not Your Father's Old Fashioned), 209

olive juice/brine
Dirty Martini, 214
Frozen Vodka Martini, 136

olive oil
Oliveto, 307

Oliveto, 307

orange bitters
14 Karrot Queen, 210
Manny's Old Fashioned, 102
Matcha Gimlet, 216
Mr. Paul's Supper Club Sazerac, 225
N.Y.F.O.F. (Not Your Father's Old Fashioned), 209

orange blossom water
Arpece, 106

orange liqueur
Aquavit Sidecar, 76
Martina Naked Ballerina #2, 24–26
Naked Ballerina #2, 23

orange liqueur, bitter
Dunbar's Numbers, 139

Orange Moon, 144

oranges/orange juice

Dreamsicle, 150
Sour Orange Juice, 43
Strive, 244
White Wine Glögg, 74–75
Young Buck, 43
O'Shaughnessy, Patrick and
Michael, 261, 303
O'Shaughnessy Distilling Co.,
11, 12, 261–264, 302–305
Oskey, Dan, 17, 270
Owamni, 10, 124–129

Pajarito, 197–200
Palmer's Bar, 131–133
Palmloma, The, 133
Parlour, 19
passion fruit liqueur
Hurricane, 226
Pineapple Passion Daiquiri,
212
passion fruit/vanilla syrup
Martina Naked Ballerina #2,
24–26
Paw-Paw Sweet Galium
Nectar
3LECHE Naked Ballerina
#2, 26–28
peach, white
Don't Sweat the Technique,
46
pear liqueur
Bonapera, 117
peppercorn simple syrup
Benny's Old Fashioned, 177
Petit Jolie l'Orange, 56
Peychauds's bitters
Hayfield, 262–263
Martina Naked Ballerina #2,
24–26
Mr. Paul's Supper Club
Sazerac, 225
Sazerac Thing, 91
piloncillo syrup/simple syrup
Mr. Paul's Supper Club
Sazerac, 225
N.Y.F.O.F. (Not Your Father's
Old Fashioned), 209
Piña Colada, 92
pine, dried white
Bashkodejiibik, 129
pineapple juice
Acapulco, 162
Aquarius, 300–301
Bonecrusher, 273
14 Karrot Queen, 210

Piña Colada, 92
Postcards from Palawan, 85
Pineapple Passion Daiquiri,
212
Polish, The, 352
Pollack, Jessi, 322–323
pomegranate juice
Natural K'Evan, 51
Postcards from Palawan, 85
Powerscourt Distillery, 266
Prosecco
Crystal Palace, 143
Sardinian Spritz, 158
P.S. Steak, 134–139
Puffed Wild Rice
Manoomin, 126
recipe, 126
Pulice, Sophia, 155
Punt e Mes
Reel-to-Reel Sling, 164–165

Quamme, Alex, 199
Quincy Cosmo, 259
Quincy Margarita, 62

Rabbit Kick, 256
Radicchio Sour
Killarney, 264–265
recipe, 264
Ratafia, Berry
Madhaus, 107
Ratafia, Bitter Almond
Arpece, 106
Red Dragon, The, 355
Red Locks Irish Whiskey,
266–269
Reel-to-Reel Sling, 164–165
Referent Horseradish Vodka,
354
resources, 30–31
rhubarb and maple leaf tea
syrup
Bourbon Street Smash, 70
rice
Manoomin, 126
Puffed Wild Rice, 126
Ube Horchata, 301
Rich Syrup
Killarney, 264–265
recipe, 265
Riva Terrace, 140–144
Roasted Tomatillo Syrup
Chupacabra, 123
recipe, 123

Rosemary Syrup
Last Corpse, 199
recipe, 278
Ruckus Rosemary, 278
Ruckus Rosemary, 278
rum
Acapulco, 162
Aquarius, 300–301
Aries, 299
Hurricane, 226
Mekarushi, 321
Next Up . . ., 82–83
Piña Colada, 92
rum, banana
Bubble Up, 182
rum, pineapple
Pineapple Passion Daiquiri,
212
rye whiskey
Benny's Old Fashioned, 177
Bonapera, 117
Hewing Old Fashioned, 87
Machine Gun Kelly Manhat-
tan, 221
Manny's Manhattan, 103
Mr. Paul's Supper Club
Sazerac, 225
The Williamsburg, 193

Saffron, 18
sage
Bashkodejiibik, 129
sake, sparkling
Dunbar's Numbers, 139
saline solution
Anne with an E, 189
Gatsby, 308
The Huntress, 186
Natural K'Evan, 51
Salt and Pepper Tincture, 40
The Gibby, 39–40
Salted Honey Syrup
Hayfield, 262–263
recipe, 263
Sardinian Spritz, 158
sarsaparilla
Manoomin, 126
Sazerac Thing, 91
Scallion Dry Vermouth,
Charred, 40
Schepker, Adam, 154–155
Schrutes and Ladders, 79
Schweigert, Peder, 302, 328–
329
Scotch

Gatsby, 308
sencha tea
  Tropical Tea, 52
Serbus, Travis, 90, 311
Sherman, Sean, 10, 12, 124–125
sherry, amontillado
  Gimlet, 324
shisho syrup
  Maravilla, 318
Shot and a Beer Back, 132
Sidebar at Surdyk's, 146–153
Siers-Rients, Ben, 90, 311
singani
  Argentine Sour, 111
Smoked Demerara Syrup
  recipe, 169
  Volstead's Old Fashioned, 169
Sooki & Mimi, 160, 162, 292, 294
Soul of the City, 222
sour cherry liqueur
  Benny's Old Fashioned, 177
  Umeboshi Sour, 274
sour mix
  Bubble Up, 182
Sour Orange Juice
  recipe, 43
  Young Buck, 43
spiceberry
  Manoomin, 126
Spicy Turmeric Gimlet, 280–281
spirits, stocking bar and, 32–33
Spoon and Stable, 322–327
St. Paul Hotel, The, 344–345
star anise
  Ube Horchata, 301
  White Wine Glögg, 74–75
Steger, Phil, 232–233
Sterling Club, 330
stocking your bar, 30–31
Strip Club, 17
Strive, 244
sugarcane juice
  Next Up . . ., 82–83
Super Lemon

3LECHE Naked Ballerina #2, 26–28
supplies and essentials, 30–31
Surdyk, Jim, 146
Surdyk, Joseph, 146
Surdyk, Molly, 146, 148
Surdyk, Taylor, 150, 153
Tabasco sauce
  Acapulco, 162
Tamarind and Thai Chile–Infused Mezcal
  Postcards from Palawan, 85
  recipe, 85
tamarind liqueur
  14 Karrot Queen, 210
Taris, Mary, 244
Tattersall Canned Cocktails, about, 33
Tattersall Cranberry Liqueur
  Soul of the City, 222
Tattersall Crème de Fleur
  Lush 75, 99
Tattersall Distilling, 270–274, 311–312
Tattersall Grapefruit Crema
  Grapefruit Negroni, 194
Tattersall Italiano
  Machine Gun Kelly Manhattan, 221
Tattersall Orange Crema
  Corpse Reviver #2, 178
  Dreamsicle, 150
  Quincy Margarita, 62
  Aquavit Sidecar, 76
Tattersall Sour Cherry Liqueur
  Benny's Old Fashioned, 177
  Umeboshi Sour, 274
tea, anise hyssop
  Madhaus, 107
tea, black
  Bulldogger Syrup, 253
  Yeah You Right, 246
tea, Earl Grey
  Madhaus, 107
tea, hibiscus
  Dunbar's Numbers, 139
tea, maple sarsaparilla
  Manoomin, 126
tea, mizu green
  Don't Sweat the Technique, 46

tea, sencha
  Tropical Tea, 52
tea, yerba maté iced
  Bonapera, 117
tequila
  Acapulco, 162
  Aries, 299
  Chupacabra, 123
  Habanero Cilantro Margarita, 200–201
  Martina Naked Ballerina #2, 24–26
  Naked Ballerina #2, 23
  The Palmloma, 133
  Quincy Margarita, 62
  see also mezcal
Terzo, 154–158
Thompson, Dana, 10
Three Olives Espresso
  Espresso Martini, 96
331 Club, 346
Tomatillo Syrup, Roasted
  Chupacabra, 123
  recipe, 123
Tony Jaros' River Garden, 351
Town Talk Diner, 17, 314–315
3LECHE, 25–27, 289–291, 294, 329, 332
3LECHE Aronia Acid
  Madhaus, 107
3LECHE Botanical Refreshers, 32
3LECHE Ispahan FBB
  Crystal Palace, 143
3LECHE Nake Ballerina #2, 26–28
3LECHE Pompelmo Fermented Botanical Beverage
  Arpece, 106
triple sec
  Lush 75, 99
Tropical Elixir
  Hurricane, 226
Tropical Tea
  recipe, 52
  Tropicalía, 52–53
Tropicalía, 52–53
Tserenbat, Billy, 44–45
Turmeric Infusion, M Vodka
  recipe, 280
  Spicy Turmeric Gimlet, 280–281
Twin Spirits Distillery, 276–281

Ube Horchata
  Aquarius, 300–301
  recipe, 301
umami bitters
  Frozen Vodka Martini, 136
Umeboshi Sour, 274
Unum "Agave" Spirit
  3LECHE Naked Ballerina
    #2, 26–28
Uyeda, Kazuo, 303

vanilla bean syrup
  Rabbit Kick, 256
vanilla extract
  N.Y.F.O.F. (Not Your Father's
    Old Fashioned), 209
vanilla mocha syrup
  Martini Espress, 149
verjus
  Arpece, 106
vermouth, Americano
  Bonapera, 117
vermouth, bianco
  Maravilla, 318
vermouth, blanc
  Dunbar's Numbers, 139
vermouth, dry
  Frozen Vodka Martini, 136
  The Gibby, 39–40
  The Huntress, 186
  Petit Jolie l'Orange, 56
vermouth, rosa
  Martina Naked Ballerina #2,
    24–26
  3LECHE Naked Ballerina
    #2, 26–28
vermouth, secco
  Bichrome Martini, 334
vermouth, sweet
  Grapefruit Negroni, 194
  Machine Gun Kelly Manhat-
    tan, 221
  Manny's Manhattan, 103
  Orange Moon, 144
  Reel-to-Reel Sling, 164–165
  The Williamsburg, 193
vodka
  about, 32
  Argentine Sour, 111
  Aries, 299
  Arpece, 106
  Bubble Up, 182
  Dirty Martini, 214

Dunbar's Numbers, 139
Espresso Martini, 59
Frozen Vodka Martini, 136
The Gibby, 39–40
M Vodka Turmeric Infusion,
  280
Martini Espress, 149
Matcha Gimlet, 216
The Northern Way, 112
Quincy Cosmo, 259
Referent Horseradish, 354
Ruckus Rosemary, 278
Salt and Pepper Tincture, 40
Soul of the City, 222
Spicy Turmeric Gimlet,
  280–281
vodka, citron
  Lush 75, 99
vodka, orange-flavored
  White Wine Glögg, 74–75
vodka, vanilla
  Espresso Martini, 96
Volcano, The, 354–355
Volstead's Emporium, 167–
  169
Volstead's Old Fashioned, 169

Wadi, Sameh, 18
Weller, Scott, 38, 43
whiskey
  about, 32
  Afternoons with Annie, 237
  Beeswax-Washed Keeper's
    Heart Whiskey, 262
  The Bulldogger, 253
  Cold-Pleated Old Fashioned,
    234
  Don't Sweat the Technique,
    46
  Hayfield, 262–263
  Irish 75, 268
  Irish Coffee, 269
  Land of Milk and Honey-
    crisp, 250
  Manny's Old Fashioned, 102
  The Mary Jackson, 243
  The Monica Helms, 249
  Orange Moon, 144
  Strive, 244
  Umeboshi Sour, 274
  The Winston Duke, 241
  Yeah You Right, 246
  see also bourbon; rye whis-
    key; Scotch
White Russian, 327

White Wine Glögg, 74–75
Williamsburg, The, 193
Winchester, Michelle, 276
wine, orange
  Dreamsicle, 150
wine, sparkling
  Irish 75, 268
wine, white
  White Wine Glögg, 74–75
Winston Duke, The, 241
Witherspoon, Adam, 104,
  144, 290, 294, 332–337
Wondrous Punch, The, 355

Yeah You Right, 246
yerba maté iced tea
  Bonapera, 117
Young Buck, 43
Young Buck Mix, 43
Young Joni, 160, 164–165
yuzu juice
  Maravilla, 318

Zappia, Marco, 19, 22–33,
  114, 268, 289–290, 294, 332
Ziaimehr, Abe, 49
Ziaimehr, Hilari, 49

—ABOUT CIDER MILL PRESS BOOK PUBLISHERS—

Good ideas ripen with time. From seed to harvest, Cider Mill Press brings fine reading, information, and entertainment together between the covers of its creatively crafted books. Our Cider Mill bears fruit twice a year, publishing a new crop of titles each spring and fall.

"Where Good Books Are Ready for Press"
501 Nelson Place
Nashville, Tennessee 37214
cidermillpress.com

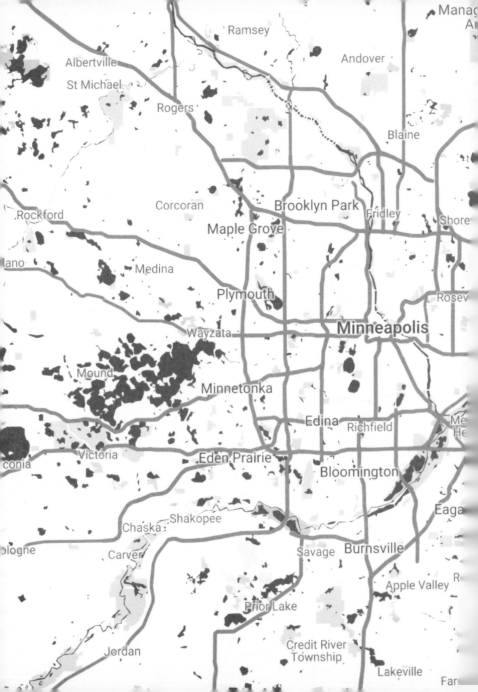